Th

On some evenings, for instance ... withdrawn from our economic horrors ... he shivers as the hunts and the hordes pass by ...
Arthur Rimbaud, *Les Illuminations*

People must not sense the truth of usurpation: it has been introduced in the past without reason; it has become reasonable; people should be made to regard it as authentic and eternal, and its beginning must remain hidden if it is not to end soon.
Blaise Pascal

THE
ECONOMIC
HORROR

Viviane Forrester

Translated from French

Polity Press

English translation © Polity Press 1999
First published in France as *L'horreur économique* © Librairie Arthème
Fayard 1996.

Published with the assistance of the Cultural Service of the
French Embassy in London.

Translated with the assistance of Sheila Malovany-Chevallier.

First published in 1999 by Polity Press
in association with Blackwell Publishers Ltd.

Editorial office:
Polity Press
65 Bridge Street
Cambridge CB2 1UR, UK

Marketing and production:
Blackwell Publishers Ltd
108 Cowley Road
Oxford OX4 1JF, UK

Published in the USA by
Blackwell Publishers Inc.
Commerce Place
350 Main Street
Malden, MA 02148, USA

ISBN 0–7456–1993–2
ISBN 0–7456–1994–0 (pbk)

A catalogue record for this book is available from the British Library and has
been applied for from the Library of Congress.

Typeset in 12 on 14 pt Berling
by Ace Filmsetting Ltd, Frome, Somerset
Printed in Great Britain by T.J. International, Padstow, Cornwall

This book is printed on acid-free paper.

I

We are living in the midst of a masterly deception, in a world gone forever, although we stubbornly insist on denying it, and while artificial policies claim to perpetuate it. Millions of human lives are devastated and annihilated by this anachronism, the outcome of persistent stratagems intended to assert the immutability of our most sacred concept the very questioning of which is taboo: work.

Twisted into the perverse form of 'employment', work is indeed the foundation stone of Western civilization, which commands the entire planet. The two seem so much a part of each other that even now, when work is vanishing into thin air, no one ever officially questions its deep-rootedness, its obviousness, still less its necessity. In theory, doesn't it order all distribution and thus all survival? The networks of exchange deriving from it seem as indisputably vital as the circulation of blood. Yet today work, regarded as our natural driving force, as the rules of the game governing our passage through this strange place from which we are all due to depart, has become an entity without substance.

Our concepts of 'work', and thus of unemployment, around which politics revolve (or claim to revolve), have become illusory, and our struggles with them are as much of a hallucination as Don Quixote's tilting at the windmills. However, we still ask the same phantasmal questions to which, as many are aware, there will be no answer other than the disaster of lives ravaged by that silence, while we seem to forget that each such life represents an individual human fate. Futile and anguishing as they are, these outdated questions enable us to side-step a source of even greater anguish: the disappearance of a world where there was still some point in asking them. A world in which these terms were based on reality. Better still: where they created such reality. The climate of that world remains in the air we breathe. We still belong to it viscerally, whether we profited or suffered from it. We are still fiddling with the vestiges of that world, busily plugging gaps, patching up emptiness, fudging up substitutes around a system that has not just collapsed but vanished.

What kind of a dream are we still made to keep on dreaming, conferring about crises in the belief that we shall emerge from the nightmare? How long before we realize we are not going through one crisis or many crises, but through a mutation? Not that of a society but the very brutal one of a civilization. We are part of a new era, and yet we are unable to envisage it. Since we do not admit or even perceive that the old era is over, we cannot mourn it, and we spend out time mummifying it instead. We insist it is still with us and in full activity, as we go on observing the ritual of a missing dynamic. What is the point of this constant projection of a virtual world, a sleep-walking society racked by artificial problems, when the one genuine problem is the fact that such problems are not at issue any more? On the contrary, they have become the norm of this both inaugural and twilight age that we refuse to acknowledge as ours.

We thus manage to uphold what has become a myth and the most sacrosanct of all: the myth that work is closely linked to all the public and private workings of our societies. We desperately carry on our exchanges, reassuring even when hostile; we perpetuate deeply engraved routines in our minds and go on singing the same old refrains, sung in the family for so long, a family now torn apart but eager to remember that it once lived together, seeking traces of a common denominator and a kind of community, even if such a community was often the source and the place of the very worst discord and infamy. Might one say eager for a sort of fatherland? For a link so organic that we prefer any disaster to the lucid perception of loss, or any risk to facing the extinction of what was once our surroundings?

Our lot is now alternative medicine, outdated pharmacopoeias, cruel operations, wholesale transfusions, most of whose beneficiaries are already healthy. Our lot is now soothing pontifications, catalogues of verbosity, the comforting appeal of the same old tunes covering up the stern, intractable silence of incapacity. We are bewitched by it all, grateful for any distraction from the terrors of vacuity, reassured by rocking ourselves to the old, rambling tunes.

But behind these masquerades, while the officialized subterfuges – these supposed 'measures' that we know in advance are not going to work – are going on, while this spectacle is swallowed hook, line and sinker, human suffering holds sway. And this is real suffering, etched in time, in what real but always concealed history is woven of. The irreversible suffering of masses of sacrificed people, which means consciences tortured and repudiated one by one.

'Unemployment' is mentioned constantly and all the time. Today, however, the term has lost its true meaning, for it covers a phenomenon quite different from the utterly obsolete one it claims to describe. Yet elaborate and usually fallacious promises are made in its name, hinting at tiny quantities of jobs acrobatically launched (at reduced wages) on the labour market. The percentages are derisory in view of the millions of people excluded from the labour market, and, at this rate, likely to remain so for decades. And by then, what kind of a state will they, society and the labour market, be in?

We can also add in some light-hearted deceptions, like the one which, in France, removed 250,000 to 300,000 unemployed from the statistics at a stroke . . . by removing from the register those who worked at least seventy-eight hours a month, i.e. less than two weeks' work and with no benefits. So simple, it just required some thinking! But notice how little the fate of the bodies and minds, masked by statistics, has not been modified, but only the mode of calculation, the way they're counted. The figures are the real point, even if they correspond to no actual number, nothing organic, no result: even if they point to nothing but a display of tricks. Trifling mischief! Like that devised some months earlier by a previous government, proclaiming its triumphant achievement in tones of amazement and self-satisfaction. Had unemployment fallen, then? No, it hadn't. On the contrary, it had risen . . . but not so fast as the year before.

While such antics amuse the gallery, however, millions of relegated individuals, and I do mean *individuals*, are entitled, for an indefinite period or perhaps until their death, to misery or the threat of it sooner or later, to the loss of a roof over their heads, to all loss of social respect, even self-respect, to the pathos of shaken or wrecked identities, to the most shameful of feelings: shame. Because they believe and are encouraged to believe themselves failed masters of their individual destinies when they are merely figures lined up arbitrarily in the statistics.

Throngs of human beings, solitary or in families, desperately struggling not to collapse, at least not to collapse too much or too fast. Not to mention the countless other human beings living in fear and danger of toppling over into that condition.

Worse than unemployment itself is the distress it brings about and the exploitation of that distress which derives to a great extent from the fact that what 'unemployment' describes is no longer valid, yet it still determines its status. The *present* problem of unemployment is no longer what the term denotes, yet solutions are claimed to be sought without reference to the fact, in the light of a destroyed past. And the jobless are judged by that very light. In fact, the contemporary form of the phenomenon known as unemployment is never delimited or defined, and thus never properly taken into account. What is designated by the terms 'unemployment' and 'the unemployed' is never really taken up. Even when this problem is supposedly the focus of general preoccupations, the real phenomenon is, on the contrary, masked.

The unemployed today are no longer put aside temporarily or occasionally, and in only some sectors; they are up against a general implosion, a phenomenon resembling those tidal waves, cyclones or tornadoes that don't aim at anyone in particular but that no one can withstand. They are subject to a world-wide logic which assumes the elimination of what is called work, that is, jobs.

However – and this discrepancy has cruel effects – social and economic life still claims to be governed by work-based exchanges, even while work itself has disappeared. The jobless, victims of its disappearance, are treated and judged by the same criteria as when jobs were abundant. They are therefore made to feel guilty for being jobless, as well as deluded and lulled by deceptive promises assuring them that an abundance of jobs will once again be available, and that soon the unfortunate consequences of untoward events will be rectified.

The result is the ruthless, passive marginalization of the vast and ever-growing number of job-seekers who, ironically, by virtue of the very fact that they are job-seekers, have actually become part of today's norm, a norm which is not accepted as such, even by those who are excluded from the job market themselves, so that they are (and are meant to be) the first to feel incompatible with a society of which they happen to be the most natural product. They are led to consider themselves unworthy of it, and above all responsible for their own situation, which they regard as degrading (since it is degraded) and even reprehensible. They accuse themselves of what they are victims of. They judge themselves through the eyes of their judges, adopting the same viewpoint that sees them as guilty and makes them wonder what inadequacies, what aptitude for failure, what ill-will or errors can have led them there. Absurd as such accusations are, general disapproval lies in wait for them. They blame themselves – and are blamed – for being destitute or for being threatened by destitution. A life from then on often

lived on public 'assistance' (and one below the poverty line
at that).

They are blamed, and they blame themselves for what is
in fact the discrepancy between the situation and our perception of it, on old opinions unfounded in the past, and
now redundant and more ponderous and absurd than ever.
All these factors – and they are far from innocuous – drive
them to feel that shame and sense of unworthiness that lead
to all submissions. Opprobrium discourages any reaction on
their part but mortified resignation.

For nothing weakens or paralyses as much as shame. It
causes radical impairment, it deadens resilience, allows all
kinds of domination, and makes easy prey of all who suffer
from it. Hence the interest of the authorities in resorting to
shame and inflicting it: it helps them to lay down the law
unopposed and break the law without fearing any protest.
Shame creates an impasse, obviating all resistance, discouraging all clarification, all demystifications or confrontations
of a situation. It distracts from everything that would enable
them to refuse disgrace and to demand a political analysis of
the situation. It also allows the exploitation of both this
resignation and the virulent panic it helps to create.

Indeed, shame should be floated on the stock markets: it is
an important element in profit.

Shame is of sterling value, as is the suffering that induces
or is induced by it. One should not then be surprised by the
unconscious, almost instinctive determination with which
its cause is permanently reconstituted or, when necessary,
mummified: a defunct and bankrupt system, indeed, but one
whose artificial continuation allows real harassment and gen-
teel tyranny to be surreptitiously put to work while safe-
guarding 'social cohesion'.

A fundamental yet never voiced question emerges from
this system: Must a person 'deserve' to live to have a right
to do so? A tiny minority, already exceptionally vested with
power, property and privileges assumed as self-evident, takes
that right for granted. As for the rest of humanity, if it is to
'deserve' to live, it must prove itself 'useful' to society or at

least to the economy that runs and dominates society; an economy more than ever merged with business, that is, the market economy. In this context 'useful' nearly always means 'profitable', that is, profitable to profit, or in a word, 'employable' (it would be in rather poor taste to say 'exploit-able').

To deserve life, therefore or rather to have a right to live depends on the 'duty' of working, of being employed, which thus becomes an imprescriptible right without which the social system would be nothing but a large-scale assassina-tion.

But what about this right to life when that system stops working, when populations are prevented from meeting this duty that gives access to life; when it becomes *impossible to fulfil the requirements*? It is well known that today access to work, to jobs, is permanently blocked off because of general incompetence, or the interests of some, or the course of history – all lumped together under the heading of fate. Is it now reasonable or even logical to demand something that is absolutely lacking? Is it even *legal* to demand what does not exist as a necessary condition of survival?

Yet this fiasco is actively being perpetuated. The norm of a gone-forever past, of a model gone flat, is still stubbornly grasped. Economic, political and social activities are still endowed with official meanings derived from phantom com-petition, from the devising of substitutes and the promised but ever-deferred distribution of something that no longer exists. We go on claiming that there is no impasse, that we only have to work our way through the few unfortunate, temporary consequences of blunders that can be rectified.

What a fraud! So many destinies are wrecked for the sole purpose of erecting the effigy of a defunct society, a society founded on work and not its absence, so many existences sacrificed to the fictitious adversary whose defeat is prom-ised, to the chimeras that they claim will be subjugated and wiped out.

How much longer will we agree to be duped, seeing no enemies except those who are pointed out to us: adversaries who have already left the field? Are we going to remain blind to the current peril, to the real pitfalls? The ship is already on the rocks but we prefer (and are encouraged) not to admit it and stay on board, sinking in the shelter of familiar surroundings rather than trying, perhaps in vain, to find our way to safety.

Thus we pursue some very strange routines. At a time when the shortage of jobs is proving to be a constant factor, ineradicable and ever-increasing, one can hardly decide whether it is more ludicrous or sinister to compel every one of the millions of unemployed to engage in an 'active and incessant search' for work that does not exist and to do so every working day of every week, every month and every year. Is it reasonable to compel them to spend hours over those days, weeks, months and sometimes years offering no less than themselves every day, every week, every month, ever year, in vain, thwarted in advance by the statistics? Does experiencing rejection every working day of every week, every month, sometimes every year, amount to an employment, a trade or a profession? Is it a position, a job, or even an apprenticeship? Is it a plausible career, a reasonable occupation, a truly commendable use of time?[1]

It seems more like a demonstration tending to prove that the rituals of work are self-perpetuating, that they still interest the interested parties who are induced by some cheerful optimism to stand in line at the windows of government employment offices where jobs are supposed to be piling up, though for the time being, curiously, adverse currents have driven them off course while only the gap left by their disappearance actually remains.

Aren't such repeated refusals and chains of rejections just a set staged to persuade the job-seekers of their nothingness?

---

[1] Do those little playlets, supposed to mime 'participation in the world of work' and a way through the sacred portals of business, really constitute any kind of professional training for the future? They usually amount to making some people on minimum benefit payment, or young unemployed, perform ill-defined and underpaid tasks, thus removing them for a brief period from those statistics which prey on the governmental mind.

To instil into the public the image of their failure, spreading the idea that the very people who are paying for the general error, for the decisions taken by some, for the blindness of all (themselves included), hold the responsibility for it and are therefore guilty, and thus punished for it? Isn't the idea to make a spectacle of their *mea culpa*, to which they too subscribe? Defeated.

So many stifled, crushed, cornered, beaten, and falling-apart lives, merely tangential to a shrinking society. A kind of increasingly opaque pane of glass stands between these dispossessed people and their contemporaries. Since they are less and less seen by others, since it is hoped that they will be even further obliterated, erased and blotted out from society, they are said to be *excluded* from it. On the contrary, they are screwed into it, incarcerated and *included* in it to the marrow. They are absorbed and eaten up by it, relegated for ever, deported where they stand, repudiated where they stand, banished, subdued, fallen – and so cumbersome, such a nuisance! They can never be wholly, sufficiently thrown out: they are included, only too clearly included, within rejection.

Is it not the way one would construct a society of slaves upon whom only slavery can confer status? Though why should a society burden itself with slaves if their labour is superfluous? At this point, as an echo to the question that 'emerged' earlier, another one comes up, one we all fear to hear: is it 'useful' to live when not profitable to profit?

Here, maybe, can be discerned the shadow, the hint, the trace of a crime. It is no trifling matter for an entire 'population' (in the sociologist's sense) to be led quietly, by a lucid and sophisticated society, to extremes of vertigo and weakness, to the frontiers of death and sometimes beyond. Nor is it a trifling matter to induce people to seek work, beg for it, any work at any price (which is to say the lowest), when they are often the very ones who would be enslaved by it. And if they do not all throw themselves body and soul into the vain search for work, public opinion thinks they ought to.

It is no trifling matter, either, for the holders of economic power, i.e., true power, to have subdued the trouble-makers who only yesterday were protesting, demonstrating, demanding and fighting. How sweet to see them beg for what they used to vilify and now regard as a Holy Grail! Nor is it a trifling matter for the economically powerful to have certain other people at their mercy: those who do have jobs and salaries and will baulk at nothing for fear of losing such rare, valuable and fragile privileges and being obliged to join the porous ranks of the destitute.

Seeing men and women taken or thrown away according to the dictates of an erratic and increasingly imaginary labour market, a shrinking market on which they and their lives depend, while it does not depend on them. Seeing, already, how seldom they *are* hired, how often they already are no longer hired; seeing how they are then vegetating, especially the young, in a state of endless vacuity, considered degrading, and how it is held against them. Seeing how, then, life treats them badly and society aids and abets in that. Seeing that beyond the exploitation of men and women there was something worse: the absence of any such exploitation. How can it not occur to us that the crowds – unexploitable, not even exploitable, no longer quite necessary for exploitation which is now in itself useless – might tremble, and each of us in the crowd?

In answer, then, to the question, 'Is it useful to live when not profitable to profit?', which itself echoes the question: 'Must a person "deserve" to live to have a right to do so?', an insidious fear arises: a widespread but justified terror that many, perhaps even most human beings, could be considered superfluous. Not inferior or even reprehended: just superfluous, and therefore harmful. And therefore . . .

No such verdict has yet been pronounced or formulated; or not even consciously thought. We are in a democracy. To most of the population, the population as a whole is still the subject of genuine interest, involving its culture and its profound affects, either acquired or spontaneous, even though an increased indifference to others is well on the way. Furthermore, let's not forget that this population as a whole votes and consumes, generating 'interest' of another kind, and inducing politicians to mobilize around the now routine problems of 'work' and 'unemployment', giving an official stamp to these false, or at any rate, badly posed problems, obscuring any appraisal of the situation and, in the short term, constantly providing the same bloodless answers to artificial questions. Not that they should be excused from finding even partial and precarious solutions – far from it. But the effect of their makeshifts is chiefly to support systems which are running out of steam as they pretend to function, however badly, and more particularly to breathe new life into obsolete power games and hierarchies.

Long experience of these routines gives us the illusion that we are to some extent in control of them, thus conferring on them an air of innocence, marking them with a certain sense of humanity, and above all surrounding them with legal barriers like so many parapets. Yes, we are in a democracy. Yet a threat is on the verge of utterance; it is already almost being whispered: 'Superfluous'.

But suppose we ceased to be in a democracy? Wouldn't this concept of superfluity (which is bound to grow) then be in danger of being put into words, stated, and thereby sanctioned? What would happen if the idea of 'deserving' to live, upon which the right to life would depend more than ever, and if the right to life itself were questioned and managed by an authoritarian regime?

Today we can no longer claim to be unaware that no horrors are impossible, that there are no limits to human decisions. From exploitation to exclusion, from exclusion to elimination, or even to disastrous, yet unknown kinds of exploitation – is that an unthinkable scenario? We know from experience that barbarity, always latent, consorts very well with the placidity of those majorities who are so good at combining the worst with the ambient blandness.

Obviously, in the face of various dangers, virtual or otherwise, the work-based system still looks like a bulwark, even when work is reduced to a shadow of itself. That may justify our regressive attachment to its outdated norms. However, the system still rests on crumbling foundations that are more porous than ever to every kind of violence and perversity. Its routines, which appear capable of moderating or delaying the worst, are going round and round in a void, lulling us into a state which I have described elsewhere as the 'violence of calm'.[2] The most dangerous violence of all, since it allows every other kind of violence to rage free, unobstructed; it stems from an array of pressures deriving from a long, a very long tradition of clandestine laws. 'The calm of individuals and societies is obtained by the practice of ancient, underlying coercive forces of such efficient violence and such efficacious violence as to pass unnoticed', so that ultimately it is no longer even necessary since it is so well integrated. The forces underlying it restrain us without any further need to manifest themselves. Nothing appears on the surface but the state of calm to which we are reduced even before birth. Lurking in the calm it has brought about, the violence lives on, active and undetectable. It watches over the scandals it conceals, consolidating them all the better, and succeeding in producing such resignation that it's no longer even clear just what we are resigned to, so well has our oblivion been contrived.

There is no weapon against such violence but accuracy and cold fact. Outright criticism is more showy but less radical, for it joins the game and takes its rules into account, thereby validating it even in opposing it. The key is to outwit: to opt out of the huge, feverish, world-wide game in which the stakes are never known, nor which show is being staged (or who is staging it), while another show entirely may be going on behind the scenes.

To arrive at establishing the facts one can never be too wary of the very existence of the problems concerned; one can never call their terms into question enough and never question enough the questions themselves. More particularly when they involve the concepts of 'work' and 'unemployment' around which are sung political chants on all

[2] Viviane Forrester, *La Violence du calme* (Paris: Seuil, 1980).

political sides and recited strings of futile, slapdash, harped-on solutions, tediously repetitive litanies of answers that we know to be inefficient, unable to undermine the accumulated distress. Nor do they aim to do so.

So – and this is the main example – the texts and speeches analysing the problems of work and therefore of unemployment really deal with nothing but the idea of profit, which is their foundation and matrix but is never mentioned. While the profit motive remains the great organizer in these scorched areas, it is kept secret. It persists upstream, further up the line, so obvious an assumption that it remains unsaid. Everything is organized, planned, prevented or induced with profit in mind, which then seems inevitable, so fused with the very fabric of life that the two cannot be told apart. It operates in full view of everyone, but unperceived. It is disseminated and active everywhere, but never referred to except in the modest guise of the 'creation of wealth' that is supposed to bring immediate benefit to the entire human race and to contain treasures of jobs.

To tamper with such wealth would thus be criminal. It must be preserved at all costs. It must not be discussed. It must be forgotten (or one must pretend to forget) that it always works to the advantage of the same small number of people always more powerful, more able to impose this profit that goes back to them as the only logical aim, the pivot of civilization and proof of democracy, the (fixed) motive behind all mobility, the nerve centre of circulation, the invisible, inaudible, sacrosanct engine that animates us.

Therefore, the priority goes to profit which is regarded as original, as a kind of 'big bang'. Only when business – that is, the market economy – has been guaranteed its share, and when that share has been subtracted, are other sectors, such as the social and political ones, taken into account, although less and less. Profit comes first; everything else falls into line afterwards. It is only later that we make do as best we can with the crumbs of the so-called 'creation of wealth' without which, we are given to understand, there would be nothing, not even those crumbs (and they are petering out anyway).

Without it there would be no reserves of work and no resources at all, or almost none.

'Kill the goose that lays the golden eggs? Heaven forbid!' my old Italian nanny used to say, and she went on to point out the necessary existence of the rich and the poor. 'We shall always need the rich. Just tell me how the poor would manage without them?' A true politician, Nanny Beppa, a great philosopher! She understood everything.

The proof? Here we are still listening – deaf to what they hatch, to the lies, the simpering of those powers my nanny revered. Powers that in any case are lying and simpering less and less, so well do they seem to have thrust their postulates, instilling their creed into the masses of globally anaesthetized people. Why bother to waste energy on winning over those who have already been disarmed, if not actually convinced, by the considerable propaganda?

Effective propaganda that has managed to appropriate a good deal of positive, seductive terminology, judiciously monopolizing, hijacking and controlling it. See the *free* market free to make a profit; see the *social* plans which are actually implemented to throw men and women out of work (and do it as cheaply as possible), thus depriving them of a livelihood and sometimes of a home. See the 'welfare', which far from providing well-being, so reluctantly and in such a miserly way alleviates the flagrant and often inhuman injustice. And among so many other expressions, those 'on the dole' who are expected to be humiliated (and are) because of their status, whereas an heir is not considered helped even though so much is doled out from cradle to grave. See *flexibility*, which ought to be called *inflexibility*, since it means savage rigidity. Flexibility denotes, among other things, the right to dismiss workers when, how and however frequently it pleases the managers.[3] Yet flexibility is

---

[3] And it often *does* please the managers, since when they make large-scale redundancies their firm's shares immediately shoot up. Don't the decision-makers themselves declare that their favourite management method is to cut labour costs – i.e., to dismiss workers?

often made out to be the best way of diminishing or even eliminating unemployment. Wouldn't this seem comic if it were not so tragic?

Innocuous indeed?

We do not hear the bell tolling for certain words any more. If those of 'work' and thus of 'unemployment' are still well embedded while empty of the very meaning they seem to carry, it is only because their sacrosanct, intimidating character helps to preserve the remnants of an organized system which may be obsolete but may still safeguard social cohesion for a while.

Many other terms, however, languish in obsolescence. 'Profit' is one, but others include 'proletariat', 'capitalism', 'exploitation' or those 'classes' now impervious to any 'struggle'. To make use of such archaisms today would be an act of heroism. Who would willingly assume the role of the corny crank, the misinformed simpleton, the country bumpkin intent upon issues about as contemporary as hunting the aurochs? Who wants to see brows not frowning angrily, but raised in incredulous amazement mingled with kindly compassion? 'You surely don't mean . . . You can't be still . . . The Berlin Wall came down, don't you know? So you liked the USSR? Stalin? But what about liberty, the free market . . . No?' And a helpless smile is bestowed on the poor retarded fool, so corny as to be endearing.

Yet the content of these forbidden words calls them back as what they cover, though remaining unexpressed, unstated, is constantly carried out. How can language take history into account without these mutilated words – when history is fraught with them, and still conveys their silent presence?

Are they banned, or have they lost their meaning, because a monstrous totalitarian system employed and even promoted them? Are we to reject outright, automatically, what others used to accept outright and automatically? Will outright automatic acceptance thus be carried on? Will Stalinism, even now it is no more, have eradicated everything, even through its very absence, using the *reductio ad absurdum* to allow silence on the part of intercessors, referees, interpreters, but also on the part of the interlocutors one has hoped for? Should it be allowed to determine this removal of words, this muteness that mutilates thinking in the midst of language? It is obvious that the authority of lacunary discourse, organized around such lacunae, forbids any analysis, any serious reflection – even more any refutation connected with what remains unsaid but is still in force.

If vocabulary, as the tool of thinking able to express events, is not only gravely suspect but is said to be without meaning, and if that most effective of threats, ridicule, is brought to bear against it, what weapons and what allies are left to those who would be saved only by a very strict appraisal of the situation – saved not so much from destitution, from an outraged existence as from being ashamed of it and from being forgotten while still alive?

How have we come by such amnesia, such laconic memories, such oblivion of the present? What has happened to make the helplessness of some and the domination of others rage so much today? How has such an acceptance by both sides, such a state, occurred? And without a conflict either, apart from the struggle claiming more and more space for a market economy which is triumphant, if not omnipotent, and which has its own logic but which no longer has any other logic opposing it any more. They all seem to share the same logic, taking it for granted that the present state of things is the natural condition, the exact point where history has been waiting for us.

No support is left for those who have nothing but loss. The only discourse heard is the deafening one of the other side. Something is hovering, totalitarian, terrifying, and with no other comments but those of Monsieur Homais,[4] more official, long-winded and pompous than ever. Monsieur Homais with his monologues. And his poison.

---

[4] Flaubert's sententious busybody in *Madame Bovary*. He is a chemist, and the poison with which Emma Bovary commits suicide is in his back room.

II

While Mr Homais triumphantly soliloquizes, with no one to oppose or even answer him for want of adequate language, we scarcely notice that we, the bit-part players, are the only ones left singing in chorus with him. Most of the real actors who took the leading roles have deserted, without our knowing it, unperceived, taking the script. We refer to them when we speak of work, or the lack of work, as if they were still present and similar to us, although within a hierarchy where they were at the top of the tree.

This is not so and never will be again.

While the spheres of employment, and even more markedly of the economy, were moving away from us, all the leading actors accompanied them. With them and like them, they became hard to discern, increasingly impalpable. If they are not beyond our range now they soon will be out of reach, lost from sight, while we still mark time on the same stage.

The fact is that we still see work in connection with the industrial age of capitalism, a period when capital had obvious guarantees: firmly established plants in easily located sites, factories, mines, banks, buildings, all rooted in our landscape and duly registered. We believe we are still living in that age when their area could be measured, their situation assessed and their costs calculated. Fortunes were kept locked up in safes. Business proceeded along channels that could be checked. Owners had a well-defined status in civil life; directors, employees and the labour force moved from one place to another, meeting and passing on real ground. One knew who the managers were, where they were, and who benefited from the profits. There was often a single man at the very top, more or less powerful, more or less competent, more or less tyrannical and more or less prosperous, owning property and managing money. He was the owner of the business (with or without equally identifiable partners). He was a tangible individual of flesh and blood, with a name, a man who had heirs and had nearly always inherited property himself. The size of his firm could be evaluated at a glance; it was known where the labour so necessary at the time was actually taking place, just as it was known where (often under scandalous conditions) both the working-class conditions and the so-called 'creation of wealth' then called profit were produced. Manufactured products, business transactions and the circulation of raw materials were of vital importance, and firms had their recognized, even certified, social rationale and function. Its configurations could be appraised, even on an international scale, and the various parts played by commerce, industry and financial strategies could be taken into account. If need be, it was easy to know whom and what to contest, thus defining the perimeters of the dispute. It all took place amongst us, in our own geographical space, to rhythms that were familiar, even when it got out of hand. And it was all expressed in our own speech and language. We were given often disastrous roles, but we were all living within the same story.

But now, the world where work and the economy merged, and where the many were indispensable to the decision-makers, has been as if blotted out. We believe we are still travelling in it, breathing its air, obeying it or ruling it, but it no longer operates, or only in make-believe, as in a children's game and under the control of the real forces which are discreetly governing it and managing its wreckage.

Gone with it too are the intermediate models which gradually took over, making the transition with the modern world: that of multinationals, transnationals, pure market economy, globalization, deregulation and virtuality. At the most, such models may still be found now in a subordinate capacity, almost extinct, and nearly always already in the power of distant and complex authorities.

As for the brand-new world dominated by cybernetics, automation and revolutionary technologies, and which now wields the power, it seems to have slipped out of our reach, entrenching itself in quasi-esoteric, sealed areas. It is no longer in step with us any more, and of course has no real links with the 'world of work' for which it has no more use and which it considers – when by chance it happens to catch a glimpse of it – as a parasitical nuisance, notable chiefly for its emotionalism, its worries and unwieldy disasters, its irrational insistence on claiming it exists. And for its uselessness, its readiness to give way, its benign character, its renunciations and its innocuousness, confined as it is to the last vestiges of a society where its roles have been abolished. There is nothing but a complete break of continuity between those two worlds. The old one is collapsing and suffering in isolation from the new one that it cannot even imagine. The new world, reserved for a caste, enters a new order of 'reality' – one might say of 'de-reality' – in which the hordes of job-seekers represent merely a wan cohort of ghosts.

Why should that caste trouble itself with the unthinking maniacs who obsessively insist on occupying concrete, tangible, clearly situated perimeters, where they can hammer in nails, fit screws, move stuff around, classify whachamacallits, calculate thingamajigs, meddle with everything and be a pain in the neck, all at a slow pace in time with human body rhythms, with laborious effort, with chronologies and tempos already consigned to oblivion? And what about their lives, their children, their health, their housing, their food, their pay, their sex, their diseases, their leisure and their rights?

How naive of them! Those whom they expect to provide everything – that is, a job – are not available any more. They are too busy in other spheres, creating virtuality, producing financial value in the form of 'derivatives' that have no more underpinning in real assets and that are proving to be volatile, unverifiable and often traded, snapped up and converted before they even come into being.

The decision-makers of our time have become what Robert Reich describes as manipulators of symbols or 'symbol analysts'[5] who no longer communicate or hardly communicate at all, even with the old world of the 'bosses') Why would they bother with so many expensive employees registered with social security, employees so unsure and troublesome compared with those hard, those pure machines outside the province of any social services, by definition easily manoeuvred and economical to boot? What's more, they are without dubious emotions, aggressive complaints or dangerous desires. They open up the way to another age which may be our age too, but we have no access to it.

This is a world living, by virtue of cybernetics and advanced technology, at the speed of immediacy, a world where speed merges with immediacy, in spaces containing no interstices, a world where ubiquity and simultaneity rule. Those who operate in it do not share that space with us, nor do they share that speed and that time, or these projects or that language, still less their thoughts or figures or numbers, even less their concern. Or the same currency.

They are not ferocious or even indifferent. They are elusive, and remember us as vague poor relations left in the past, in the burdensome world of work and 'jobs'. If our paths cross, they are not too proud to wave to us from their own world, before going back to join one another in those fascinating games that condition this planet whose existence in the end they know only on their networks. They govern the globalized economy, transcending all frontiers and all governments. Nations for them are like town councils.

And it is in that very empire that the workers, poor devils, imagine that they still can find a place for their 'labour market'. One could die from laughing! It was once enough

[5] Robert B. Reich, *The Work of Nations: Preparing Ourselves for 21st-Century Capitalism* (New York: Alfred A. Knopf, Inc., 1991).

for them to know their place; now they must learn to have no place at all. That is the message being hinted to them, although still very discreetly, a message that no one wishes or dares to decipher, for fear of imagining its possible consequences.

None the less, such is the way we are going. A great number of human beings is already unnecessary to the small number who shape the economy and therefore hold power. Crowds of human beings thus find themselves, according to the logic now in force, without any reasonable reason to live in this world, yet a world into which they were born.[6]

To obtain the ability to live and the means to do so, they would have to fulfil the requirements of the networks that rule the planet, that is the markets. However, they do not meet those requirements, or rather, the markets no longer respond to their presence and no longer need them, or only a very few of them, fewer all the time. Therefore, their lives are not 'legitimate', only tolerated. Their existence is unwelcome, granted out of sheer indulgence and sentimentality, through antiquated reflexes, in memory of what was long considered sacred (theoretically, at least), also for fear of scandal, and because of the advantages the markets can still derive from such lives; and for reasons of political jousts and the electoral stakes based on a fraud, the assumption that this is a temporary 'crisis' that all parties claim they can halt.

Moreover, a certain atavistic mental block prevents our accepting such an implosion straight away. It is difficult to admit, unthinkable to state, that the presence of a multitude of human beings is becoming precarious, not because of the ineluctability of death but because, although they are alive, their existence is not in line with the prevailing logic, for it no longer brings profit but instead is proving expensive, too

---

[6] Crowds of people on other continents are experiencing this lack of status. It looked as if their future would bring them closer to the conditions of Western life. It remains to be seen whether the great majority of people in the world will not have to adapt to *their* conditions instead.

expensive. No one in a democracy will dare to say that life is not a right, or that a multitude of living people is surplus to requirements. But mightn't one dare to say so under a totalitarian regime? Hasn't it been dared already? And do we not already admit the principle ourselves, while deploring it, when famine decimates populations no further away from us than we might go on holiday?

The privations suffered today by a considerable and increasing number of individuals might well be mere preliminaries to the rejection (which might become a radical one) of those who endure them, for they are not due to weaken or decrease, as is unconvincingly claimed in political statements that are all talk and no action. They are due to weaken or at least to push aside those who are their victims. Economic discourse (all action but no talk) is heading that way: in its terms, the masses are vague abstractions, and no one takes much notice of the disparities except to deal at the lowest level possible with the few poor social gains acquired by the more fragile elements among those masses, who are soon to be 'excluded' even further – or rather, even further *included* in their dispossession.

If there is not much space left, and if what *is* left keeps shrinking because of the decline of employment – while society itself is still based on employment, and human survival still depends on it – its disappearance in no way troubles the real powers, those of the free market. However, the destitution caused by that disappearance is not either what they aim at. They find it rather a drawback put in their way, but one they might as well take advantage of, since it is well known that profit can often profit from poverty. What matters to them, and all else pales beside it, are the money supplies, the financial gambling including speculations, new kinds of transactions, impalpable flows, and this virtual reality, the most influential of all today.

It has to be admitted that from their point of view this is only common sense. The present situation and its attendant phenomena are perfectly suited to their aptitudes, their professional duties, even their ethics. Then again, the intox-

icating and 'human, all too human'[7] passion for power and
gain finds both its source and the grounds where it can take
off and flourish, irresistible, ravenous and devouring. Those
who share this power find their natural roles in such a
context; the drama lies in the fact that all the other roles are
left by the wayside.

A long, a very long and very patient, secret and surrepti-
tious process conducted in the shadows must have led to
that abandonment which has facilitated the hegemony of a
now anonymous private economy, grouped by means of
massive mergers on a world-wide scale into intricate networks, so inextricable, mobile and ubiquitous that it is difficult to locate them. They thus evade everything that could
restrain, oversee or even observe them.

This phenomenon should be studied some day, and the
clandestine history of that imperceptible yet radical evolution established.

What can be assessed today is the extent of the progress
made by private powers, largely due to the extent of prodigious communications networks, instantaneous exchanges
and the ubiquity deriving from them. These powers were
the first to draw on such developments and the first to
exploit them, thereby abolishing time and distance (no insig-
nificant feat) to their own advantage.

The result is a staggering proliferation in the number of
wide-ranging assets they can embrace, dominate, combine
and duplicate without a thought for any laws or constraints
that they are easily able to bypass in so global a context.

They need not bother much about states, which compared
to themselves are often so powerless and helpless and en-
tangled in legalities and contestation, put in the hot seat,
while the private economic powers can forge ahead free,
more motivated, more mobile and far more influential than
any state and without any electoral preoccupations, political
responsibilities or other controlling factors, or of course any
moral cares about the people they are crushing. They leave it

[7] Nietzsche.

to others to demonstrate that they are being crushed for
their own good, in fact for everyone's good, since obviously
the good of all derives from the 'goods' of those very powers.

They can override political authorities, and need not take
account of any broken-down ethics or any sentiments. Ultimately, in the higher reaches of their own spheres, where
the game becomes imponderable, they no longer have to
answer for success or failure and have nothing at stake but
themselves and their transactions and speculations, which
are endlessly renewed for no other purpose than their own
movements.

They encounter no other obstacles than the ferocious ones
set in their path by their peers. However, the latter are
following the same path towards the same goals, and it
makes no difference to the system if some of them try to
reach certain of those goals before or instead of others. In
such complex networks, their frantic rivalry actually welds
them together, bending their energies more keenly on the
same ends within a common ideology. An ideology never
stated or acknowledged, but still in action.

Therefore such private, transnational economic networks
are increasingly dominating the powers of states; far from
being controlled by the countries, the networks control them
and form, in fact, a kind of nation themselves. A nation
without territory or governmental institutions but increasingly in command of the institutions and policies of various
countries, often through weighty and prominent organizations such as the World Bank, the IMF[8] and the OECD.[9]

An example: private economic powers often have control
over national debts. As a result, states depend on them and
are under their thumb. These states do not hesitate to con-
vert the debts of their protectors into public debts, for which
they then assume liability. The debts will then be honoured
by the citizens, with no compensation in return. Ironically,
once the debts of the private sector have been recycled in the

---

[8] International Monetary Fund.
[9] Organization for Economic Cooperation and Development.

public sector, they increase the national debt by an equivalent amount, thus placing the state even more firmly under the control of the private economy. This private economy, taken over by the state, as is often the case, and thus by the community, is never considered as being 'on the dole'!

Here we see the private economy given unprecedented freedom – that very freedom it has insistently claimed and which expresses itself through legalized deregulations and official anarchy. A freedom vested with any number of rights and total permissiveness: unbridled, its logic permeates a waning civilization whose wreckage it is accelerating.

Such a collapse is camouflaged, put down to temporary 'crises', so that a new, emergent form of civilization will arrive unnoticed, a civilization in which only a very small percentage of the world's population will find it has any functions. Yet it is on such functions that everyone's way of life depends, even more everyone's ability to live – in other words, that the prolongation, or otherwise, of every human life also depends.

Centuries of tradition say that a fundamental principle is at work here: without a function no one has any place in life, any obvious access to it, or at least to its continuation. Now, today, such functions are irrevocably disappearing, yet the principle is still in force, although it will no longer be able to organize society but only to destroy the status of human beings and damage or even decimate them.

No one is bold enough to admit or envisage such a peril, still less to mention it. A very grave omission, and literally vital – or mortal – since it means that no one then faces the obscured menace, or opposes it or tries to reverse the current, still less to pinpoint and expose the creed behind these sinister virtualities. No one suggests attempting to devise some lucid way of management that perhaps might offer everyone a place, but within a world where it would be acknowledged that the rules have changed. Instead, those who depend on a defunct system are buried alive with it. Such pathos and disaster could be avoided, and perhaps even without harming the protagonists and profiteers of the new creed.

A creed which is never articulated, but that it would be blasphemy to dispute. Doubt is implicit in faith, but forbidden in the economic *diktat*. Suppose you venture on a few timid reservations expressing some alarm at the prospect of the hegemony of a globalized abstract and inhuman economy? You will soon be shut up by the dogmas of that same hegemony – in which, let's be realistic, we seem to be trapped. You will soon be brought up against the laws of competition and the competitive spirit, adjustment to international economic rules – which are those of deregulation – and you will soon hear the praises of a flexible labour force sung. Take care not even to whisper some shy remarks hinting this might be the way to make labour more subject than ever to the whims of speculation and the decision-makers, in a world which must be profitable on *every* level, a world which is reduced to nothing but a vast corporation – not necessarily managed by competent persons either. Some might call it a vast casino. You will soon find the respect of those mysterious and more or less clandestine laws of competition mustered against you, and imposed on you. As a finishing touch, you will find yourself blackmailed with threats of relocation of companies and investments, or with the more or less legal transfer of capital, all of which happen anyway.

Blackmail: the trap is tightening.

This discourse, these threats brutally dealt out on groups already weakened, whose critical faculties and lucidity are being more or less surreptitiously reduced, meet, if not with the approval, at least with the tacit, mute consent of a stunned society.

But we are deaf to that silence, which becomes the best accomplice in the business expansion now permeating our planet to the detriment of human life: The pre-eminence of balance sheets is becoming universal law, a dogma, a sacred postulate. And it is with the logic of the righteous, the impassive benevolence of kind souls and virtuous minds or the seriousness of theoreticians that there is an ever-growing number of human beings despoiled, in destitution, deprived of their means, their rights curtailed, and their health wrecked, their bodies exposed to cold and hunger, to blank hours and horrified lives.

No resentment, no hostility have imposed that situation; no feeling, no scruple have prevented it, nor any compassion. No indignation or anger have opposed it. It seems to respond to a sense of fatality, which in line with the workings of the human mind, leads to even worse abuse of the underprivileged, punishing them for the very contempt they attract and above all forgetting all about them. Even so, they are in the way. What is to be done with the droves that do not even protest any more (or only in the face of a *fait accompli*) but are still standing around? How gladly we could do without these wet blankets, these leeches, in fact these profiteers who wish themselves to be indispensable and claim they exist rightfully! How irritating is the loss of time and finance they still induce. Life could be so comfortable, spent just among ourselves! But being 'among ourselves' soon might mean for many (for most?) people finding themselves gathered 'among ourselves' perhaps, but within the sacrificed group – growing by leaps and bounds – they have had to join.

So here they are, the 'excluded', but who are, as a matter of fact, more deeply included than anyone. One has to put up with them, which means endlessly repeating and wildly sowing pious wishes, refrains, leitmotifs and clichés that sound in the end like tics. Unemployment will have to be described as 'our prime concern' and the return of employment as 'our priority'. Once it will have been said, reiterated and hammered home, then only reflections, deliberations and decisions will be allowed to concentrate solely on the financial flows, under the aegis of its prime movers and disregarding all other contemporaries – that is to say, most people now alive – except as unavoidable factors or as credulous categories to be treated in the most anaemic way, accentuating their low profile. No one would dare to suggest that they have little *raison d'être* left and represent mere burdens or weights dragging their bodies as importunate entities.

A proliferation of parasites with no reference justifying their existence but for the traditional presence of human crowds on the earth's surface – a tradition which is coming to be judged as retrograde.

We haven't reached that stage yet? Well, look, for instance, at a luxurious, modern, sophisticated city, Paris, where so many people, the old or the new poor, sleep in the streets, their bodies and minds wrecked by lack of nourishment, warmth, care, also togetherness and respect. Ask yourself how far the wretchedness of such lives shortens them,[10] and whether walls or watch-towers are needed to imprison these people, or weapons to threaten their lives. Note the ferocious indifference surrounding them, or even the general disapproval turned against them. That being only one example among a multitude of barbaric aberrations very close to us geographically, indeed our near neighbours, established among our own affectations. All that is called 'social fracture'. Not social injustice, or social scandal, not social hell. No: social fracture.

[10] 'The statistical level of premature death (i.e. before the age of 65) varies according to social class . . . and shows a clear hierarchy. The rate of premature death among manual labourers is 2.7 higher than among the senior executives and liberal professions, and 1.8 higher than among the middle executives and shopkeepers.' This is scandalous in itself but what, then, is the rate of premature death among the homeless? (Inserm, SC8, in *INSEE Première*, February 1996; Inserm is the French equivalent of the Medical Research Council and the US National Institutes of Health).

III

Paris, you may say – what about Paris? Look at it: a city like many others. Pedestrians walking about, cars driving down the streets. Look at the shops, the theatres, museums, restaurants, the offices, the government ministries. All in working order. Holidays, elections, news items, weekends, the press, bistros. Do you hear the faintest groan, the smallest curse uttered? Do you often see tears shed or meet people weeping in the streets? Have you noticed any ruins? Stores are selling merchandise, books are being published, fashions are paraded down the catwalk, festivities are celebrated, justice is dispensed. There are people at play from the Comédie Française to the Roland Garros stadium. It is as pleasant as ever to stroll through the markets – not the financial ones but the markets for flowers, cheese, spices, game. Civilization is imperturbable.

Yes, there are beggars. Cardboard boxes are their homes, the pavement is their bed. Destitution lurks in the corners. But life goes on: civil, gentle, elegant, even erotic. Store windows, tourists, clothes, some trees, appointments – none of that is finished nor is it about to end.

Is that so? Of course if we take life and its landscapes as they appear or are presented to us, if we stick to the authorized, not to say recommended viewpoint, and to the line we are encouraged to take, if we agree with the idea that the privileged will always get further privileges and others will be cast aside, if we follow the beaten track in the corrected order, if we go to the point of approving what we are supposed to leave alone – then indeed we shall perceive nothing but the harmony thus concocted. We shall have welcomed and absorbed the picture of a world in tune with its inhabitants, or rather with an ever-decreasing number of them (but we shall have been provided with every possible means of dismissing that from our minds, along with any concern it may cause). We shall have benefited from all the subterfuges designed to convince us that whoever we are, we are not, and never will be, on the side of sheer misfortune.

We shall have evaded even the slightest questions about the others. We shall have ignored the fact that while Paris, like all big cities, has its samples of poverty on display, the bulk of poverty is relegated to forgotten ghettos in poor suburbs, to housing estates adjacent to the city but more alien to it than any foreign city, more distant from it than another continent. We shall have obeyed the prohibition which separates us from stagnant distress simultaneous with our own lives. We shall have forgotten how long, slow and agonizing is the distillation of misery in the veins. We shall not have detected the humiliating pain of being the fifth wheel, a nuisance; nor shall we have felt the terror of inadequacy, the obsession and the heaviness of want, or the wearisome sense of being regarded as an embarrassment, even by oneself.

We shall not know what it is like when young to have one's energies instantly, endlessly, permanently disregarded and mutilated. We shall not know what it is like when old to feel such tiredness with nowhere to rest, and of course, no right to any well-being or regard. We shall ignore the distress of the socially excluded and of those threatened with social exclusion. We forget, or will soon forget that each of them desperately clings to a name and a conscience, if not always to a fixed abode. Each of them is a prey of that body that must be fed, sheltered, cared for, kept alive and which is such a grievous burden. There they all are, with

their ages, their hands, their hair, their veins, the complex
delicacy of their nervous systems, their genitals, their stom-
achs. With their deteriorated lives. For each of them, there
has been a birth that meant for each of them the start of
that life that has led them there.

See that old man, for instance, worn out, defeated, mis-
used, broken, terrified for so long, coerced for so long, who
doesn't even beg. See that look of utter old age ingrained by
destitution even into young faces, even the faces of infants.
See the faces of those babies on other continents in times of
famine, of those babies with the faces of old men, with
Auschwitz faces, cast straight into privation, suffering and
the throes of poverty. They seem to know and to have
known all about human history from the first and to be
better versed than anyone in the science of centuries, as if
they had already experienced and acknowledged everything
about the world that rejects them.

Look at the eyes of indigent adults, indigent old people –
but can their age even be determined? Meeting those eyes is
even more unbearable when, as might happen, some kind
of expectation survives in them: often there is no worse fear
or anguish than hope. And no worse horror than to know
your life is ended long before your death, and must be
dragged about for the rest of your days. Failed steps with no
route any more and yet this route has to be taken. Such
faces, such bodies of persons who are no longer regarded as
persons, remembering the person they once were and what
that person they had in charge or believed they had has
become. Does one then remember and dwell on the traces
of these seasons when everything drifted away, when everything froze into resignation? Does one visit again and again
these insidiously slow periods during which one has become one of those who are overlooked and disregarded
even when seen, not listened to even when heard, and who
keep silent anyway? One of those unworthy of considera-
tion or recognition, except as phantoms of folk legend, with
no right to be fleshed out in whole words, only (in French,
at least) labelled by acronyms, the ghosts of words. Such

French acronyms include SDF[11], RMI[12], or SMICards[13] or nothing at all.

The danger increases with anonymity. Those initials confirm consignment to insignificance, emphasize the loss of a name and of any recognition of privacy on which the sense of individuality, and thus of equality and legal rights is based. They sanction the mutilation of the past, the obliteration of any biography, now reduced to a few capital letters designating no characteristics even of a negative nature, much like the brand-marks on herds of cattle. Acronyms make the inadmissible banal by putting it into pre-ordained categories, under sets of mute letters which leave the unbearable unsaid, and deal with scandal by rubber-stamping it.

Such acronyms do not denote the status of someone officially occupying a position – for instance like the CEO. Instead, acronyms, anonymity lead to the normalization of social annulment or, better still – if one may say so – to the registration of that annulment. Such acronyms show that someone has sunk without trace among the outcast, among the absent who are all supposed to be similar within a definition which defines nothing. No details are to be found here, no trace, no comment. Nobody is left here so that nothing will happen anymore to anybody. Calm is restored. Oblivion sets in, the oblivion of a present already put on record and indexed. The distance from other people increases, and even more the distance others keep from *you*, so as to escape the fear that some day they may become part of the pile. Who wants to identify with shadows who have been left no identity of their own?

Such mass anonymity is found, in great multiples, in the immense crowds abandoned on other continents, where at times whole populations are delivered over to famine, epidemic disease and all forms of genocide, in countries often under the rule of potentates approved and maintained by

[11] SDF: homeless.
[12] RMI: a minimum social income.
[13] SMIC: minimum wage; SMICards: people on minimum wage.

the great powers. See the teeming throngs of Africa, of South America, the poverty of the Indian subcontinent, and so many other places. And facing this suffering on a monstrous scale, see how the West remains indifferent to the slow death and hecatombs happening no further away than the distance we might travel to an ordinary tourist destination.

However, this indifference to the crowds of living people being sacrificed is interrupted from time to time by a moment's emotion when the television screen shows one or two images of these derelictions and tortures, while we discreetly relish our sense of magnanimous indignation, the generosity of our emotions, of our pangs underlaid by our even more discreet satisfaction in being only spectators, and in control.

Only spectators? Yes. But we *are* spectators, therefore witnesses. We *are* informed. Faces and scenes, hordes of starving people, of deportees, massacres reach our armchairs and sofas, sometimes live through TV screens and sandwiched between two commercials.

Our passivity, our indifference to this distant horror but also to horrors nearby (fewer in number but no less painful) may bode the worst danger. They seem to protect us from general misfortune by keeping us apart from it, but that in itself makes us vulnerable and puts us in danger. For we are in danger, at the very heart of it. Disaster is in progress, a very specific one. Its chief weapon is its quick insertion, its ability to arouse no alarm, to seem natural and self-evident, to make it seem obvious that there is no alternative, never to be imagined before the logic that could oppose its grip or even denounce its own logic has been defused and curbed.

In such a context, the homeless, the excluded, the entire disparate mass of those shunted aside are perhaps the embryonic form of the crowds that might constitute our future societies if the present patterns are carried on.

Moreover, isn't it odd to regard as a virtual monstrosity in our prosperous regions situations corresponding to the current condition of entire populations on other, underdeveloped continents? Can the breaking wave of poverty endemic to such areas invade our sophisticated lands? Can anything so 'unseemly' become possible in a society which is far from naive, and indeed well informed, with refined critical apparatus, highly acute social sciences, and a distinct taste for analysing its own history? But is it not for the same reason and out of satiation, cynicism and disillusionment, sometimes out of conviction but often out of negligence, that society is not disposed to abrasive ideas and so little aware of the urgent need for lucidity?

After all, some may say, in an internationalized, delocalized and deregulated context, why should some countries still be privileged? Is not equity the fashion?

But let's be serious. The scandal is that, far from seeing hard-hit areas emerge from disaster to join the prosperous nations – as might have been expected – as one might have thought could be expected – we are witnessing the establishment of that disaster infiltrating societies that were until now expanding, and anyway as rich as they used to be, but where the methods of acquiring profit have changed, some would say progressed. In any case those methods are shown up in their increased capacity for one-way appropriation, concentrated on an ever-attenuated number of beneficiaries, while the active presence of other players formerly thought necessary and thus remunerated is also declining.

So true is it that a country's wealth does not necessarily make it prosperous. It consists of the wealth of some people, a few whose properties are only apparently located there, or part of the assets of a national body of finance. In fact, they belong to a quite different kind of organization, a quite different order, run by the lobbies of globalization. It flows only into that economy, which is light-years away from any country's official policy, as well as from the well-being or even survival of its inhabitants.

It's always the same phenomenon: powerful people in small numbers no longer needing the labour of others, while those others (are we their keepers?) can get lost and take their states of mind and health reports elsewhere. Alas, there is no elsewhere, not in life on this earth, even for true believers. We have no alternative geography, no other ground, and it is always the same lands on the same planet that hold both the gardens and the charnel houses.

IV

Indifference is ferocious: it represents the most active and most potent party. It allows all manner of exactions, the most fatal and sordid of deviations, as the twentieth century, tragically, has shown.

Achieving general indifference is more of a victory for a system than gaining partial support, even on a large scale. In fact it is indifference that allows certain regimes to attract massive support, with known consequences.

Indifference is nearly always a majority and unrestrained reaction. Recent years have been champions of peaceful blindness to the setting up of absolute control; champions of camouflaged history of advances gone unnoticed, of widespread inattention. Such inattention that the inattention itself is not even noticed. There is no doubt that lack of interest, of observation has been the result of silent, persistent strategies slowly to smuggle Trojan horses into place, and so cleverly to be based on what they spread – i.e., the lack of vigilance – that they themselves are and remain undetectable, and all the more effective for it.

So effective that the political and economic landscapes have been able to metamorphose in full view of all, but unperceived by anyone, without attracting attention, still less arousing concern. The new global pattern was able to invade and dominate our lives unnoticed, except by those economic powers that established it. Here we are, then, in a

new world, ruled by those powers in accordance with un-
tried systems, and within which, however, we act and react
as if nothing had happened, as we go on daydreaming in
accord with an organization and economy no longer operative.

Detachment and drowsiness have been so dominant that
if, by chance, we now suggest to stem some political or social
procedure, some 'politically correct' act of piracy, we discover that the projects we meant to oppose are firmly in
place, have been devised at length and in detail further up
the line while we were dozing, so that they are the only ones
conforming to the only principles now in operation and
appear to be deeply rooted, ineluctable, and often quietly
settled and in place.

Everything has been staged for so long by the time we
intervene, or believe we do so. Any point of protest has been
evacuated. We are not even faced with the *fait accompli*; we
are already locked within it.

Our passivity leaves us caught in the meshes of a political
net covering the world-wide landscape. The issue is not so
much the positive or fatal value of the policies which pre-
sided over this inventory as the fact that such a system could
impose itself as a dogma, without rocking the boat or calling
for any comment apart from a few, rare, belated ones. Yet, it
has invaded both physical and virtual space, establishing the
absolute pre-eminence of the markets and their fluctuations;
it has appropriated and purloined wealth to an unprecedented degree, placing it out of reach, even invalidating it by
expressing it in symbols which themselves are at the heart of
abstract deals eluding all exchanges other than virtual.

However, we are still engaged in trying to patch up an outdated system no longer valid, although we hold it responsible for the ravages actually inflicted by the establishment of
the new, omnipresent system. The advantages some find in
seeing our attention thus distracted from what is instigated
encourages them to promote and prolong the general fraud.

It is not so much the situation that endangers us – it could
be modified – but it is precisely our own blind acquiescence

and general resignation to what is presented as ineluctable. Indeed, the consequences of this global management are disturbing, but the fear is a vague one, and most of those who feel it do not know where it comes from. We question the secondary effects of globalization (unemployment, for instance), without going back to the phenomenon itself and blaming its coercion instead of accepting it as a fate. The history of that coercion seems to rise from the depths of time; we cannot date it, and it seems destined to hold sway for ever. Its devouring actuality is seen in the perfect tense: it takes place because it *has* taken place! 'Everything moves with time', writes Pascal. 'Custom is the whole of equity for the sole reason that it is accepted. That is the mystical basis of its authority. Whoever tries to trace it back to its origin destroys it.'

However, a genuine revolution was and is at stake and has managed to establish the neo-liberal system, to embody it, activate it and make it able to invalidate any logic other than its own, now the only one in operation.

Without any spectacular or even visible upheaval, a new regime has taken over. It is dominant, sovereign, and wields such absolute authority that there is no need to make any display of it, so obvious is it in the facts. A new but regressive regime returning to nineteenth-century concepts, but one from which the labour factor would have disappeared. Shudders!

The present neo-liberal system is flexible and transparent enough to adapt to national differences, but 'globalized' enough to confine them progressively to the status of folklore. Stern, tyrannical but diffuse, hard to detect but all-pervasive, the new, unproclaimed regime holds all the keys to the economy, which it reduces to the spheres of business, which make haste to absorb everything that did not already belong to that sphere.

Of course the private economy owned the weapons of power long before these upheavals began, but its present power derives from the new breadth of its autonomy. The populations which were once indispensable and could exert pressure by uniting so as to weaken and oppose it are increasingly useless now and have hardly any effect.

As for the weapons of power, the private economy never lost its hold on them. Although it was sometimes defeated or threatened with defeat in the past, even then it managed to preserve its tools intact, more particularly wealth, property and finance. If by force and temporarily it had to part with some of its advantages, they were always greatly inferior to those it did not give up.

Even at the time of its more or less short-lived defeats, it never ceased undermining the enemy positions with unparalleled and even very valiant tenacity. Perhaps that is where it rejuvenated itself, drawing nourishment from its setbacks if necessary, taking refuge in obscurity and camouflaging itself while refurbishing those weapons it had retained, polishing up its doctrines and consolidating its networks. Its order has always endured. The model it represents might have been repudiated, trodden under foot, held up to public obloquy, might even have appeared to collapse – it was never more than in abeyance. The predominance of the private spheres and their dominant classes were always re-established in the end.

The fact is that power is not the same as might. Might cares nothing for mere 'powers' or prerogatives, often granted and delegated by itself with a view to managing them better. Might has never changed sides. The leading classes of the private economy have sometimes lost power, but never lost might. A might Pascal calls *force*: 'Empire founded on opinion and imagination will reign for a time, such an empire is mild and voluntary. Empire founded on force reigns for ever. Opinion is thus like the queen of the world, but force is its tyrant.'

– Those classes (or castes) never ceased to be active, to supplant others, to be on the watch, or to be sought-after, and tempting, holders of lures. Their privileges have always been the object of most people's daydreams and desires, wished even by many of those who genuinely claimed to oppose them. Nothing could ever separate them from the tools of power such as money, occupation of strategic positions, ability to distribute appointments and to forge bonds with other powerful people, control of trade, prestige, the right knowledge and know-how, ease and luxury. They have permanently kept the dominance not always conferred by power, but inherent in might.

Today, there are no limits to that dominance. It has taken over everything, above all those modes of thought constantly brought up short by the logic of an organization so well set up by a force whose mark is omnipresent and that is ready to award itself everything. But didn't everything already belong to it? Isn't it appropriating places to which it already held the keys? And aren't those keys meant to keep the rest of the population it doesn't need any more out of the limitless areas it regards as its own?

In practice this potency is such, its grip is so firm, its power of saturation so efficient, that nothing outside its own logic is viable or able to function. Outside the neo-liberal club there is no salvation. Governments know that, bowing to what is incontestably an ideology, although it is denied and even more so as that ideology's specificity consists in disclaiming and condemning the very principle of ideology.

Nevertheless, the era of neo-liberalism is in place and has managed to impose its philosophy without ever having had to formulate it or set out its doctrine, so active and embodied was that philosophy even before being noticed. Its ascendancy runs a domineering and indeed totalitarian system, although for the moment it is set within democracy and is therefore tempered, limited, whispered and snug, with nothing showy or proclaimed about it. Indeed, we are within the violence of calm.

Calm and violence within logical structures leading to postulates resting on a principle of omission: destitution is left out of the calculations, and so are the destitute it has created and sacrificed in a pompous, offhand manner.

The effects of this self-contained system and its silent procedures often turn out to be criminal, even murderous. In our regions, however, the aggressive nature of such calm violence is expressed through abandon. People are allowed to pine away and perish. The responsibility for these defeats is laid on those who stumble, the discreet cohorts of those without a job who are supposed to have one, required to get one, enjoined to find one while it is common knowledge that the source has dried up.

The same old story again!

Lists of the unfortunate that will very soon become lists of the blameworthy. The burden they carry makes them burdens themselves, reducing them to the role of those 'others' who have always been mistreated at minimum expense, but if they make demands, argue, struggle, refuse to comply or become militant, they cause amazement. How can one of the 'others' be so lacking in aesthetic feeling as to disturb the pervading harmony? How can he be so lacking in moral sense as to disturb the voluptuous drowsiness? How can he be so lacking in a sense of citizenship that he does not understand the interests of those who oppress him with such a clear conscience? How can he be so immodest as to put himself forward? He is only injuring himself, since 'they' were acting for his own good ('they' being firmly and sincerely convinced that what is good for them is good for the general good).

It is true that representatives of the 'others' have always been regarded as suspect, as inferior (which goes without saying, and is naturally, indeed, the very heart and substance of the creed), as threatening too, and as valuable only for the services they once rendered and now hardly render at all, and will render less and less, for there will be almost no services left for them to render. Is it surprising that their value keeps falling closer to zero?

Here are revealed the real feelings of those who dominate any regime for the 'others', and the basis on which they are calculated. Soon and – alas – with increasing frequency, it will be discovered how, according to such calculations, once zero is reached, exclusion leads to expulsion.

It is a vertiginous slope. Torment at the loss of employment is felt on every level of the social scale. On every level, it is a crushing blow which seems to violate the identity of the person affected. He or she immediately feels a sense of imbalance and wrongly of humiliation, then soon of danger. The executives can suffer at least as much as unskilled workers. It is astonishing to find how quickly one can lose a footing, how stern society then becomes and how soon there is no one and nothing to turn to, or almost nothing. Everything fails, closing in and moving away at the same time. Everything becomes shaky, even one's home. The street is coming closer. There is hardly anything that cannot be done to those who no longer have the 'means'. Above all, they can't expect to be spared in any area.

So the winding-up process of social foreclosure sets in. The general, glaring absence of rationality is accentuated. What reasonable correlation can there be, for instance, between losing a job and being evicted and thrown into the street? The punishment is on an altogether different scale from what is given as its obvious motive. If one thinks about it, it is surprising enough that being unable to pay, unable to pay any more, unable to manage to pay should be treated as a crime. But to punish so harshly, to throw people out into the street because they are not in a position to pay rent as they are out of a job, when jobs are obviously officially lacking or because the jobs they do have are too low-paid for the appalling price of too scarce housing. All this comes close to madness or deliberate perversity. Particularly when having a home is a condition of keeping or finding the work which alone would enable you to find a home again.

The pavement is the answer. Pavement which is less hard or insensitive than our present systems.

This is not merely unjust but distressingly absurd and ludicrously stupid. It makes a mockery of the complacent style of our allegedly civilized societies, unless it denounces some very well-managed interests. In any case one could die from shame. But who exactly suffers shame, sometimes death, always a damaged life?

An absence of rationality? Here are some examples.

Exempting the fortunate managing classes from blame –

leaving them out of the picture for once – but accusing certain underprivileged groups of being a little less underprivileged than others – in short, of being a little less victimized – making victimization the example to conform to and victimization the norm.

— Regarding those who do have work, even if underpaid, as privileged people, profiteers in a way. Hence giving unemployment as the norm. Also to be indignant at the 'selfishness' of workers, these satraps who are reluctant to share their work, even when underpaid, with those who have none, while failing to extend such demands for solidarity to the sharing of fortune or profit which – today anyway – would be considered moronic, obsolete, and moreover in quite bad taste!

On the other hand, it is perfectly fitting, even commendable, to vituperate against the 'privileges' of such habitués of luxury hotels as, for instance, railway workers who are blessed with more acceptable pensions than some other groups, such a derisory advantage compared to the unlimited, unquestioned favours the truly privileged grant themselves as a matter of course. Very suitable, also, to cast aspersions on those dangerous predators and notorious plutocrats, workers or employees who venture to ask for a rise in the wages that are already regarded as suspect signs of shameless splendours. It is most enlightening to compare in the same newspaper the total amount of the rise – which will lead to fierce argument, be revised downwards and sometimes be refused – with the price quoted as most reasonable in the dining-out column of a single restaurant meal, costing only three or four times more than the monthly rise requested.

One more example: very appropriate too – and for a long time – to set a section of the country's population against another, alleged to be shamefully favoured (public service agents, low-level government employees), but no account is taken of the really privileged except to describe them as big business and to depict this big business, the directors of multinationals merged with small business companies, as the only people who will dare to take risks, as adventurous souls always and endlessly eager to put themselves in danger, ever anxious to risk . . . one doesn't quite know what, while such nabobs as underground drivers and such inveterate upstarts as postal workers scandalously prosper in all security!

Big business is supposed to have in its possession and to create employment, while even when subsidized, granted exemptions and generally mollycoddled for that purpose, not only does it create no jobs, or very few (and often at such cheap rates that it creates the working poor), but even when the beneficiary, partly thanks to the advantages mentioned above, it sacks workers left, right and centre.

Yet business leaders now seem suddenly to relegate musicians, painters, writers, scientists and other jesters to the role of dead weights, not even counting all the other human beings all invited to raise humble and dazzled glances at such constellations.

As for these usurpers wallowing shamelessly in job security, their immunity to the panic created by the instability, the fragility, the disappearance of this unemployment is seen as a scandalous danger in itself. Worse still, they slow down the asphyxiation of the labour market while asphyxia and panic are the breasts of economy in its fulfilling modernity, and the best guarantors of 'social cohesion'.

Would unemployment, thus, be public friend number one?

Isn't it somewhat surprising that a country like France, where so much genuine poverty is exhibited and spreading (and the same goes for other advanced countries), that country so proud of its *Restos du coeur*[14] (whose necessity amounts to an accusation) nevertheless still dares to proclaim itself the fourth economic world power. And isn't it surprising to see this fourth-ranking world power strutting and swaggering while disengaging itself as far as possible (but less than in many other advanced countries) from problems

[14] Soup kitchens, 'Restaurants of the Heart', a charitable organization created by Coluche, a popular comedian.

of health, education, housing and so forth, decreeing as an excuse, while deploring it, that they are 'unprofitable'?

We shouldn't want it to be held against us to appear so excessively rational, materialistic and coarse as to wonder what results emerge from the exporting sprees and surges in the balance of payments that obviously make the country quiver with pride to be Power Number Four – to be one down from the podium, surrounded by the cardboard shelters inhabited by the homeless and by rising unemployment curves and falling consumption graphs. Not that any of this seems to have much influence on life in cottages or urban areas.

Yet it does have a lot of influence on the lives of many groups, business networks and other financial operators, and on the lives of their leaders who, from where they stand, are absolutely right to be pleased with and enjoy their lives in what is, after all, a most licit way.

They have the attractions of lucidity on their side, and very logically pursue their own logic, their own interests, with that admirable faculty and enviable wisdom enabling them not to worry about situations engendering destitution. They become sensitive to it only when coming across it in a novel or a show. Then and only then, while reading or watching, do they feel moved or indignant with all the force of their usually quiescent generosity, for as long as they are actually reading or watching. They do not see poverty and injustice; they do not recognize them as intolerable or take them seriously except as part of an entertainment. Then and only then will they espouse such subjects, getting delectable and well-controlled emotions out of them.

Let's take Hugo's *Les Misérables*, as an example. Cosette and her mother move these people to tears on the screen, the stage, the page of a book, and so does Gavroche, whom they would loathe in real life. The most cruel, the most exploitative and the most indifferent of the exploiters identify with the oppressed or their protectors. But who identifies with the Thénardiers? No one! And yet . . . All the same . . . No! You must be joking! They are – we all are Cosette,

Gavroche. At the worst Jean Valjean. And even, thinking of it, rather Jean Valjean. They all are ... we all are Jean Valjeans.

The capitalist utopia has been achieved during the lifetime of these decision-makers. Why shouldn't they rejoice? Their satisfaction goes without saying and is only human. Too much so? That's none of their business – which is confined to business. Anyway, they have hardly any time to stop and think about it, anxious as they always are to aim at increasing their profits. In their eyes, to be fair, profit means success.

Theirs is a fascinating world; they have an intoxicating vision of it, and one that works thanks to its despotic re-duction. While fatal, it still makes sense for those who are part of it. However, its logic, its undoubted intelligence lead, inevitably, to the disaster of its hegemony. Whatever its skilful displays of hypocrisy may be, its powers are put to its own service, to the service of that arrogance which makes it regard what is profitable to itself as good for everyone and find only natural for a subordinate world to be sacrificed to it.

Here, again, they are perfectly right and owe it to them-selves to exploit such a favourable situation, such a blessed period, ours, in which no theory, no credible group, no mode of thought or serious action opposes them any more.

It all allows us to witness masterpieces of persuasive strat-egy which successfully convince us that policies leading to or even accelerating social disaster and pauperization, to the detriment of an immense majority, are not just the only possible ones but also the only desirable ones – and first of all, for that majority.

A first argument, like a familiar refrain, is the redundant and ever-magical promise of 'job creation'. A notoriously empty and utterly blighted formula, nevertheless inescap-able, because no longer lying on the subject might soon mean no longer believing in it, and having to wake up and find oneself in a nightmare belonging to neither sleep nor even waking fantasy. It might soon mean being compelled to face the brutal reality, the immediate, contingent danger and torments of emergency, and also maybe the panic of 'too-lateness' when facing a general, global clamp-down. A planetary one, at that.

And with no weapons to face it, unless lucidity, a sense of precision, the demands of attention and the effort of intelligence are potential weapons which might at least enable everyone to achieve autonomy, and not to adopt the point of view of others, but instead see, evaluate and recognize themselves through their very own vision.

Ceasing to integrate other people's judgements, ceasing to appropriate them would mean ceasing to accept their verdict as evident and condemning oneself on their behalf. A first step would then be achieved away from that shame imposed on the unemployed, for instance. It might lead away from all subordination.

A step, perhaps the only one, but not a solution. Solutions won't be sought here. Seeking them is the lot of politicians who, prisoners of the short term, become their hostages. Their voting public demands at least the promise of rapid solutions, and politicians distribute them with largesse. Far be it from us to let them get out of looking and finding solutions. But do they ever do anything besides hastily attacking some superficial detail which, once patched up at best, will allow greater toleration of the general malaise – a malaise, a misfortune which will stagnate, often blurrier than ever, being better masked by that very detail?

Using solutions as blackmail alters the problems, hinders any lucidity and paralyses criticism, which can now be easily answered in tones of kindly irony: 'Yes, yes . . . and what do you suggest?' Nothing! The speaker suspected it, reassured in advance: without an at least possible, envisaged solution, the problem disappears. To pose it would then only be irrational, and even more the slightest comment or criticism.

A solution? Perhaps there is none. Is it a reason not to try and review what is scandalizing or to understand what we are going through? A reason for not acquiring at least that kind of dignity? Alas, conventional wisdom considers it obviously immoral, daft and absurd blasphemy or heresy to insist on considering a problem if the presence of a solution is not given as certain.

Hence so many rigged and slapdash 'solutions', so many problems obscured, denied, silenced and buried, so many questions censored.

Indeed, there may well be an absence of solution – but an absence of solution most often means that the question has not been well put, or that the problem is not where it was thought to be.

Demanding the certainty of at least a virtual solution before taking a question into account amounts to replacing it by a postulate and distorting that very question which thus dodges the inevitable obstacles and discouraging effects it might have run into. Even when avoided, such obstacles do not disappear, they persist, insidious, censored, under cover, even more deeply rooted and dangerous since they have been side-stepped. Circumventing, avoiding and disguising becomes the main concern, while the essential will not be tackled at all, or even worse, it will be regarded as resolved.

Above all, the criticism of the question itself will have been dodged, the possibility of an absence of any way out will have been avoided, which would have forced us to concentrate on the situation instead of being distracted by improbable solutions not even glimpsed but supposed to exist. Bitterness and intolerable anxieties of the present will have been escaped, while the fabric of that present will have been neglected and its potential threats censored. The major deception which makes us linger on false problems so that the real questions cannot be asked will remain undiscovered and able to persist.

By avoiding these questions we spare ourselves for now the revelation of the worst. But doesn't fearing the revelation of the worst lead to being even more crushingly thrown into it? Doesn't it lead to going on struggling with ever-waning strength, and without even knowing within or against what the struggling takes place?

Isn't it terrifying to remain so passive, as if paralysed and frozen in the face of problems upon which our survival depends? For one of the real questions consists of asking ourselves whether our survival is part of the programme or not!

(Yet the political machine works to divert and suppress such questions; it mobilizes to converge on other, specious issues, directing public opinion to them and thus keeping it in abeyance, focused on false problems.

Attention is more thoroughly distracted when it turns to the phenomenon, which is even more vital (or mortal) than generally assumed, of the disappearance of employment and the artificial extension of its hold over all our data. Challenging the false questions, re-posing those that were shunned, denouncing the dodged ones, eliminating those arbitrarily reintroduced (and given as capital whereas they are no longer valid) – only this would unveil the essential, urgent and barely glimpsed questions. Asking the real questions would expose the duplicity of the current powers, or rather potencies, and their interest in seeing society remain in thrall to an outdated system based on employment.

An even greater interest that grows in these times, complacently called times of 'crisis', crisis whose effects are so beneficial for the markets: paralysed populations brought into line by panic, labour and services to be had for almost nothing, and governments enslaved to an all-powerful private economy, or at least more dependent on it than ever.

Interests served by emergency 'solutions' most often grafted onto a rotten situation that has neither been defined nor analysed, still less reviewed, but made to persist as is. The utter failure of those artificial, fudged, bungled 'solutions' then goes to show that there is only one answer to such problems, and it consists of leaving everything to rot in the *status quo*.

The real emergency suggests that facts should be reviewed, since they alone escape the most radical prohibition: the perception of a permanently blotted-out present. Only the facts will cast a crude, bright light on things that are usually hidden and thus allow manipulation. It is by identifying an issue so as to study it taken in its very movement, in its very flight, within its very disguises and contradictions that we can see it as it really is: unadulterated and not buried under preconceived ideas or artificial corollaries.

Failing fictitious solutions, perhaps we shall then have a chance of approaching the real problems at last, instead of those which have been used to lead us astray. Only by a break with the ruses of perfunctory versions, artificial perceptions, and imposed simulacra can we look at the situation in which we are really involved. We may then try to cast light on it or – no certainty whatsoever – resolve it. At least we shall have discovered what is at issue and above all what traps are to be avoided: like fake problems and rigged scenarios. From that point on and from that point only – will it be possible to fight fate or to fight for a fate. To acquire, or recover, the ability to lead that fate even if it means being subjected to it, even if it proves disastrous.

V

Such a fate with its suppleness, its tremors, its weight of hope and fears, the inklings of a future, is precisely what is refused, what is denied to so many young people, girls and boys, prevented from inhabiting the society such as it is imposed on them as the only viable one, the only respectable one, the only authorized one. The only one on offer, yet offered like a mirage, since while being the only licit one it is forbidden to them and being the only one in service, it rejects them. The only one to surround them, it remains out of their reach. These are the paradoxes of a society based on 'work', that is, employment, while the labour market is not just declining but is perishing.

Paradoxes that exist in exacerbated form in poor suburban areas. For if obtaining work proves to be difficult for most people and almost hopeless for many, others – and first those called 'the young', understood as being from the 'hot', poor suburbs – have none or almost no chance of having a right to it. Always the same phenomenon: that of a sole way of survival, foreclosed

For these young people, predestined for this problem, fused with it, there is no way out of the disaster and no limits to it, even illusory. A dense and by now almost traditional network forbids them from acquiring any legal means of making a living, but also any authorized reason for living at all. Marginalized by their status, which is geographically defined even before their birth, condemned straight away, they are *the* quintessential 'socially excluded' and the true masters of the art of being excluded. After all, don't they live in places designed and planned as ghettos – once ghettos for the working classes, now for the unemployed and aimless? Don't their very addresses indicate one of these no man's lands shown as such and considered as 'land of no man'? Or 'land of those who are not men', or even 'non-men'. Areas which seem to have been scientifically created for people to collapse in them. Waste lands indeed!

These youngsters, who will not always keep representing youth, who will become adults, who will grow old if life gives them a chance to live, will have – like other human beings – to bear the weight (always such a heavy one) of the future lying ahead. Theirs is a vacant one, where everything society holds as positive (or presented as such by society) has already been as if systematically suppressed. What can they expect of the future? What will their old age be like if they ever reach it?

The moorings are immediate, in injustice and flagrant inequality without those concerned being responsible, without their having put themselves in this situation. Their limits were fixed before their birth. And the corollary of that birth is rebuffs, relegation of a more or less tacit character, linked to great indifference.

An indifference from which society wakes each time in panic and alarm: 'they' are not integrating, 'they' do not accept everything with the good grace we have a right to expect – at least not without struggling, not without outbursts, useless in any case, not without infractions of a system that casts them out, incarcerates them into eviction. Nor either without responding to the permanent, latent aggression which is their lot, with aggressions even more brutal, obvious and explosive as they occur, almost always and necessarily, in their 'own' circumscribed space. Whether they are born and bred French or French of foreign origin or are foreigners, 'they' are squeezed in an unstated yet factual segregation and are still indecent enough not to integrate.

But integrate with what? With unemployment, with destitution? With rejection? With the vacuity of boredom?
With a sense of being useless, even a parasite? With an
aimless future? Integrate! But with which group of the unwanted? With what degree of poverty, what kinds of hard-
ships, what marks of contempt? Does it mean integrating
with hierarchies which will immediately put you on the
most humiliating level without your having been given the
chance, without ever giving you the chance to prove yourself? Does it mean integrating with a social order which as a
matter of course denies you any right to respect? With the
implicit law which says that poor people should be allowed
lives of poor people, have the interests of the poor (meaning
no interests) and work suitable for the poor (if there is any
work to be had)?

To distinguish here between born-and-bred French and
children of immigrants, with a right or not to claim French
citizenship, would be to fall into one of those traps set to
divert our attention from the essentials, so as to divide in
order to rule. The real issue is that of *poor people*. And that of
poverty.

Racism and xenophobia that are brought to bear on young
people (or indeed adults) of foreign origin serve to distract us
from the real problem, that of destitution and penury. 'Social exclusion' is ascribed to differences of colour, national-
ity, religion and culture, which supposedly have nothing to
do with market laws. But the socially excluded are the poor,
as it has been always and forever. The poor and poverty.
Even if poor people are set against poor people, the oppressed against the oppressed instead of against the oppres-
sors, against what is oppressing, poverty is what is really
targeted, bullied and repudiated. Has anyone ever heard of
an Emir expelled from a country, handcuffed and tied to the
seat on a charter plane?

Indeed, it is the poor who are immediately regarded as
undesirable, immediately relegated to where there is only
want and confiscation: relegated to those landscapes both
so close and so incompatible as these poor suburbs have

become, as they have been allowed to become, and where a part of those not needed any more have been dumped, and thus put aside, set up in these masterpieces of slow death. In those ostracized places which as a whole manifest emptiness and the absence of what is found elsewhere, of what is not there, while that absence makes one all the more aware of it. Décors of what is lacking. Places of removal but ones that can also be, have to be, the scenes of habits, of intimacy and memory. They are barren places which, oddly enough, would suit anchorites and the ascetic life. Such stripped-down, discouraged and discouraging surroundings, the obvious symbols of an alienation and melancholy which they both display and cause, conveying and embodying it.

Here in this emptiness and endless vacuity human lives are caged and fall apart, energies are drowned, trajectories annulled. Those whose youth is trapped here, powerless, are aware of it and would rather not think about the rest of their lives. One of them, on being asked, 'How do you see yourself in ten years' time?' Replied, 'I don't even see myself at the end of this week![15]

Is it possible to imagine what they must feel in the slow tedium of their days, with no right to any of the things held up to them as making up life, and what they must feel about being regarded not only as devoid of any value but simply non-existent in relation to the values they have been taught? Yet when they are not enthusiastic about these values or the education that transmits them they are met by amazement.

Why should they take offence, public opinion wonders. Since they are the poor, isn't it natural for them to be poor? Since this is where they live, isn't it natural for them to be there?

So unfavourable and widespread is the prejudice against them that these young men and women are blamed for living in such areas. Just notice how their difficulties in finding work are compounded when they have to give their address. The point is not to present them as angels or deny the

---

[15] *Saga-cités*, broadcast on France 3, 10 February 1996.

existence of delinquency and criminality, but that there is tunnel vision on both sides, their own side and the side that relegates them. Insecurity? But what else is inflicted on them? Let's admit they are each of them guilty of what they make of their situation, but they did not get themselves into it, and still less did they choose it. They were not the architects of the lethal places where they live, or the decision-makers who planned, approved and commissioned them, who allowed them. They are not the despots who invented unemployment and eradicated that work that fails them and their families. They are only those who are more penalized than anyone else for not having any.

The damage they do is visible, but what about the damage they suffer? Their existence functions as a confused, endless nightmare, resulting from a society organized without them, around their more or less implicit rejection.

But cynicism leads all powers to resent those they oppress. And this suits us, since the general conviction is that social misfortune is a punishment. And so it is – an iniquitous one.

Having scruples about the devastated lives of these young (and not so young) people is not a common experience for them. The scruples are for these young, ashamed of being spurned.

In this genuinely unspeakable context, there is no denying their brutality and violence. But what about the ravages they have been subjected to? What about these annulled destinies, deteriorated youth and abolished future?

Their reactions, their fighting back are resented. Yet in truth, despite or because of their delinquency, they are in a position of absolute weakness, of isolation and are forced into total acceptance if not consent. Their struggles are merely those of trapped animals, already defeated and aware of it if only from experience. They have no 'means', caught in an all powerful system where they have no place, but from which they haven't the faculty to remove themselves either, more rooted than anyone else among those who want them to go to hell and who don't bother to hide it. They are, and know they are, without work or money or future. All energy wasted. Hence, they are the prey of a subterranean, effervescent pain boiling with rage at the same time as it crushes them down.

Imagine youth, your youth, that of those close to you, spent in this way (which is beginning to spread to all levels of society, but is muted, more latent and less fatal the higher up it goes). The only legal options are closed to them. Even anxiety is useless when there is no hope, when the future appears identical to the present, without plans, and old age the same. When life is calling out to them, when nothing has been even hinted to them about the richness that their one luxury might hold for them: their so-called 'free time'. A time that could really prove free, thrilling and making them vibrate while instead it oppresses them, ruins the hours, and becomes their enemy.

Perhaps the worst scandal of all lies in the confiscation of those values, forbidden nowadays – let's name them: cultural values, those of intelligence – which are outlawed, for they do not open 'windows of opportunity', but even more, because they risk introducing energizing elements into a system leading to lethargy, and encouraging a state that might be described as close to death throes.

Yet the discredit they apply to themselves may seem quite as scandalous, trapped within scorn with no respect ever shown to them or to their families. And caught in that shame, more or less repressed as hatred, that even when repressed does not prevent them from being stripped from the very start or considering themselves so, by the mere fact of existing. Like so many victims, they are led to blame themselves, seeing themselves through the belittling eyes of others and joining those who blame them.

How can one believe that they could, that they can refuse to be paralysed in this most subaltern condition, and that they could deny its validity or criticize the fate laid down on them without appearing to be subversive? Without seeming to oppose that fate in a stupid, nasty way? And who would support them? What group? What texts, what ideas would?

They can only shake their lot off in devious, often violent and illegal ways which debilitate them further, and which, in a way, fulfil the wishes of those who have an interest in leaving them aside, since doing so thus seems justified now.

Nevertheless, these outcasts, these left-overs thrown on the social scrap heap are expected to behave as good citizens destined to a full civic life brimming with duties and rights, while instead they are left with no chance to fulfil any duty, and while their rights, already much curtailed, are casually scorned. How sad then and how disappointing it is to see them infringe the codes of good behaviour, the mastery of social graces, the rules of etiquette of those who edge them out, look down on them, jostle and scorn them as a matter of course! How deplorable that they will not adopt the good manners of a society which so generously manifests its allergy to their presence and helps them see themselves as done for!

Whom are they kidding?

And who's kidding whom with the offer of silly, worthless occupations under various schemes on the pretext of employment? The latest idea[16] is to get them to police their own tower blocks among (or rather against) their own people, without actually being police officers, and again on the cheap. This would not be far from official informing, and would seem very close to cleverly concocted gang warfare. Not to worry: like so many others, that plan of plans will be forgotten tomorrow. Yet this constant harping will have swayed the media, people's minds, and filled the time. The imagination of the authorities has no limits when it comes to playing to the gallery with idiotic makeshifts that have either no effect or a harmless one on anything.

Least of all do they have any effect on these young people, surrounded by a bleak dream-like world, within its pallid relentlessness, its absence of openings, where the only values officially promoted are those of civic morality mostly linked with work – so they have no means of following them – or of

---

[16] In France, spring 1996.

the virtues, made sacred by advertising, of merchandise which they have no means of acquiring either, at least not legally.

Excluded from what is demanded of them, and thus from an eventual desire to respond to it, they can only invent other codes valid in a closed world, out of sync and disruptive. Or they can get caught up in forms of delirium, the disaster of terrorism. The temptation of being terrorism's proletariat. Of being the proletarians of something. This is the situation.

What do they stand to lose, since they have not received anything but patterns of life that everything prevents them from imitating? Patterns produced and imposed by a society without making it possible to conform to them. The impossibility of reproducing the criteria of circles which are forbidden to them and reject them is immediately catalogued as a defection or outright refusal, a sign of utter unfitness, proof of their anomaly and the perfect pretext for continuing to deny them and disown them. To forget them there, abandoned and banned.

Done for!

This is where we reach the peaks of absurdity and programmed thoughtlessness. Sadness, too. For there they are, excluded like their elders (and in principle their descendants) from a society based on a system that no longer functions, but outside which there is neither status nor salvation. At least within legality.

Perhaps they represent for that society the very image of its own death throes, still disguised and delayed: the picture of what the disappearance of work produces in a society that is bent on basing its only criteria, its foundation on it. Very likely that panic-stricken society sees them as the image of its future, and that image subconsciously received as a premonition accentuates its state of tension. Above all, it meets with a strong desire to declare itself and believe itself different from its marginalized members.

Perhaps the image of this youth illustrates what that anxious society fears for itself when surrounding them with what are now only its traces, but yet maintains them in the hollow of an almost abolished system from which at the same time it repudiates them.

Here they are, anchored in repudiation, facing nothingness, that vertigo due to stationary deportations into prisonlike spaces yet without tangible walls, hence in spaces from which they cannot break out, the absence of physical barriers precluding escape.

There they are, in that effervescent age, with superannuated dreams and useless nostalgia, with a desperate desire, masked by hatred, for that expired society that they will probably have been the last to be deluded by. Those expelled from it and living, banned, on its borders are alone (or almost) in still seeing it as a Promised Land. As in a bad novel, love and its delusions grow and are exacerbated when facing the beloved's refusal.

So it goes with some of these youngsters, perhaps with all of them, possessed by a mad dream: the dream of integrating a society which is geographically close to them but inaccessible to their biographies. Many of them – many more than one might think – ache to be able to daze and dream that dream, this time a precise one, hence even more unreal: the dream of acquiring a job. A job as the Holy Grail! But they are not at all of the Niebelungen[17] type; they are rather of the Bovary type. Yes, the Emma type. Here they are, avid as she is for what ought to be and is not, but was, if not promised, recounted and celebrated. Avid for what is the fabric of dreams and is lacking. Here they are, like Emma, refusing to accept the absence of what is escaping, that is yet imagined to exist elsewhere, but is never encountered and never happening – and without which nothing exists infinitely but an ocean of endless boredom. And also as far as the eyes can see, loss. Loss within the society of the 'haves'.

There they are, the preys of absence, prisoners of lacunae, coveting something that does not exist and, like Emma, frustrated by a programme that is all the more excellent for

---

[17] Teutonic legend.

being fanciful. They find themselves without status as she
found herself without love. Deprived of what they believed
was real and due to them, they debauch themselves as she
did. They try to mime what they vainly desire, and as she
did, they caricature it. Unless society itself is a caricature of
what life could be, ought to be, of what it would, after all, be
reasonable that it was. Of what Flaubert himself expected
life to be. Gustave Flaubert, an accomplice of Madame
Bovary's dreams. Madame Bovary, of whom Flaubert said of
himself: 'Madame Bovary, c'est moi.'

So they steal, as Emma ran up debts; they take drugs, as
she made love, all in pursuit of something held up to them as
obtainable, desirable, necessary and certain, although it
never was. Imprisoned as she was in days that 'began their
same old procession again,' they hope for 'endless twists of
fate',[18] and like Emma they try to find a part to play, and a
major one, even if one outside the code and the law. Like
her, they will have compromised themselves, struggled in
vain, to end up as she did, logically defeated. While once
again and perhaps for ever, Homais's morality spreads out-
ward as he and his like go on, honoured, covered with
decorations, perorating, supposedly sheltering the poison
they hold.

Above all, they are supposed to cover up the planetary
horror by their pompous, pontificating speeches and rehash-
ing so as to make us indifferent to it. Better still, so that we
become deaf and blind and inaccessible also to that beauty so
often produced within that magical horror, by the heroism
of human beings' struggle. A struggle not so much against
death as a struggle to miss, with even greater fervour, that
strange, greedy miracle of life. That wonderful ability to
invent themselves, to exploit the brief interval they are
granted. The unspeakable beauty often provided by their
insane ambition to manage that Apocalypse, to detect, to
construct structures or, better still, to work out, to chisel a
detail; even better, to insert their own existence into the

---

[18] Gustave Flaubert, *Madame Bovary*. [trans.]

mass of disappearances. To participate with odds and ends in a certain continuum, even if a deplorable one, while tied up in the order of time, their bodies and their breath are all, from the cradle to the grave and in chaos, abolished in advance and on the road to destruction. Stoicism that enables life not to be a preface to death. Or not to be only that.

VI

A parenthesis here, but it will not take us far from the 'hot' and poor suburban area problems or from those whose more or less knowingly falsified versions are disclosed with disconcerting facility, like so much poison, anaesthetized as we are by the tedious repetitions of the many Homais, whose true business is to deafen and numb everyone.

On the other hand, the business of culture is among other things to induce criticism of their imbecilic pedantry and provide the means of doing so. To have something else heard beyond, if only silence. Learning to hear silence, allowing its sounds to reach us, perceiving its languages, letting sound come through, defining some meanings, and new meanings, means disengaging oneself a little from the ambient babble, to be less trapped in a rut; it means giving some space to thinking.

Indeed, thinking cannot be learnt. It is the most shared, the most spontaneous, the most organic process there is. But also one from which we are the most led astray. Thinking can be unlearnt. Everything conspires to that end. To indulge in thinking even calls for boldness when everything opposes it, and first of all often ourselves. Engaging in thought demands some practice such as forgetting its reputation for being austere, arduous, unpleasant, inert, elitist, paralysing and endlessly boring. Or such as outwitting the ruses that try to convince one of the gap between intellect and guts, thought and emotion. If one manages to outwit them, it certainly looks very much like salvation! And it may allow everyone to become – for better or worse – a true inhabitant of that world by right, whatever his or her social status. No wonder thinking is not encouraged much.

For nothing is more rousing than thought. Far from representing a gloomy resignation, it is the very quintessence of action. There is no more subversive activity than thinking, none more feared, more slandered, and this is not due to chance, nor is it innocuous. Thinking is political. And not only political thinking is, far from it. The mere *fact* of thinking is political. Hence the insidious battle, led more efficiently than ever today, against the *ability to think*, which, however, represents and will increasingly represent our only recourse.

I have written elsewhere[19] – and will summarize here – how in 1978 during a colloquium at Graz in Austria, when one of the speakers asked the very international audience whether they knew Mallarmé, 'a French poet', the whole audience burst out laughing. Imagine not knowing Mallarmé! Later, an Italian speaker expressed his indignation at that laughter. He also mentioned some proper names. 'Do you know them?' We knew none of them. They were those of machine gun brands. He was back from a country he cited as an example, a country in the throes of civil war where '90 per cent of the people' knew those brand names, while 0 per cent of them knew that of Mallarmé. Hence we were all elitist, affected snobs, in short, 'intellectuals'. We had no sense of real values; our own were futile, narcissistic, narrow-minded and useless. Still, there were battles to be fought. Urgent ones. He contemplated us with disgust, with wrath in his eyes. Humble and sheepish – all the more since the colloquium's theme, to compound our infamy, was 'Literature and the pleasure principle!' – the hall gave him an ovation.

Something made me uneasy, I rose to speak and heard

[19] *La Violence du calme.*

myself saying that it might not be desirable to find it quite natural for an immense, a huge majority to have no other choice but to be ignorant of Mallarmé. A majority that had not chosen not to read him, but that had had no chance whatsoever to read him or even know his name. While our very denigrator showed he was no stranger to that name since he was able to deplore our erudition.

Yet within the immense majority of social groups removed from the name of Mallarmé, there was the same proportion of men and women as in our so disastrously minoratarian group able to read Mallarmé and find out whether or not they enjoyed it. They had not, like us, had access to the training and information leading to the knowledge of his existence and the liberty to choose whether or not to read him, and having read him to appreciate him or not.

If the servant of the machine gun, if the peasants of Africa (and I heard myself repeating a now obsolete list, as mentioned by our friend), if the miners of Chile, if most of the unskilled labourers of Europe (today we would say the unemployed[20]) knew nothing of Mallarmé or what leads to his name, it was not of their own will; they had no access to him. And great care was taken everywhere that they should get no such access. For them the machine guns. For others the leisure to enjoy or not reading Mallarmé.

Now something would change at long last (I heard myself continuing) if the peasants of Africa had the means to choose by themselves their own spheres of knowledge and make their decisions in line with the many options open to

---

[20] Today, almost twenty years later, our friend could ask another question, and would not need to travel abroad to do so: he need only tour the employment agencies. In France, he would meet with a specific culture within which the people seeking those elusive jobs move. A culture into which they alone, or almost alone, are initiated (but there are many of them, there are more and more of them). A culture which turns out to be more esoteric than any page of Stéphane Mallarmé! The culture of the forests of acronyms. 'Do you know', he might ask, 'the meaning of PAIO, PAQUE, RAC, DDTE, FSE, FAS, AUD, CDL, among so many others?' And what would you have replied?

us. Was it a virtue to be ignorant of the name of Mallarmé but not of a machine gun? We could attempt to decide. Our friend was deciding for them. They could not do so: they didn't have this latitude, that right. Which we had.

Weren't the leaders of political movements on all sides – or of both sides in the case of a specific conflict – closer to each other, more qualified for exchanges among themselves, than they were with their partisans, with each one of them, and their hired guns – in short, with the men behind the machine guns?

The systems that more or less slowly, more or less obviously, more or less tragically lead to dead ends would be far more endangered and their power much better controlled if Mallarmé had more readers, or at least more potential ones. The powers are not mistaken here: they know very well where the danger lies. If a totalitarian regime is ushered in, the first thing it instinctively does is to seek out its Mallarmés and suppress them or send them into exile, however small their audience.

The work of Mallarmé is *not* elitist. It tends to break the straitjacket hampering us, to decipher language, its signs and its discourse, and thereby makes us less deaf and blind to all that is hidden from us. It tends to extend our personal space, exercise, refine thought and make it flexible – thought alone enabling criticism and lucidity, those powerful weapons.

Machine guns are violent, sometimes indispensable if disaster is to be avoided, but their violence is anticipated; it is part of the game, and almost always serves the eternal recurrence of the same changes. The terms will have been moved without changing the equation. History consists of these fits and starts. Meanwhile, the hierarchy flourishes.

To have read Mallarmé presupposes the acquisition of certain abilities which could lead to certain faculties, and thus to the approach to certain rights. They may also lead to the ability not to respond to the system in the reductive terms that are all it offers and that squash contradiction. And to the ability to denounce the demented version of a world in which we are caught and paralysed, while the authorities who deliberately set it up complain of having to run it.

But whatever the side the powers may be on, so as to better indoctrinate, manipulate, and subjugate populations, the human organism must be diverted from the arduous, visceral, dangerous practice of thinking, and the search for exactitude, that rarity, must be shunned. Once reserved for only a few, the practice of thought will preserve their power.

Mallarmé, I heard myself concluding . . .

That's when a man in the audience exclaimed, 'Mallarmé is a machine gun!'

He was right, too.

I let him have the last word.

VII

Among those youngsters, those young inhabitants of what are called the 'hot' areas, names of machine guns do not replace that of Mallarmé. Emptiness does. Emptiness and the absence of any plans, any future, any happiness, even as an aim, or the slightest hope. Yet a certain knowledge might compensate for this void and even induces a certain pleasure in treading those paths that lead to the name of Mallarmé.

Let's not fool ourselves!

But isn't the one luxury these people own their free time? And couldn't it allow them to make forays into these effervescent regions? Instead it allows them nothing, for they are tied within a rigid, run-down system which imposes on them exactly what it denies them: a life linked to wage-earning and dependent on it, what is called a 'useful' life, the only one approved and accepted, and that they will not lead as it is less and less viable even for others, and no longer at all for them. Nevertheless, its fantasy confines them in an existence ruled by the vacuity brought about by its absence.

This all weighs heavily, very heavily in the meagre squalor of the poor suburbs.

At the other pole lies a teeming, effervescent world, delectable but underrated and perhaps on its way out too (it is true that it always was and that this is one of its characteristics): not of the jet-set world but a world of research, thought, wit and fervour. The world of the intellect, a term rejected with deliberate scorn concerted and encouraged by society, as witness the knowing winks of any fool who, pronouncing the word like an insult, expects tacit agreement and instant sniggers. And there is nothing innocent about it.

Many of these youngsters at a loose end would be as much inclined as anyone to enter the world of the intellect, if only they had the keys to it. They even are more available to it than most, since they have more of that time that could be free but instead becomes vacant, empty enough to blow one's brains out, time full of shame and loss, while time is the most precious element of all. Whereas with time as a starting point, their lives could be lived to the fullest.

But supposing, imagining it possible, would be regarded as the height of absurdity, especially as the most basic education is already one of the worst experiences for these young people, who are so marginal (or marginalized) that one doesn't willingly venture into their territories, ignorant of the codes in force there, and they seldom venture into most of ours.

Those areas and their inhabitants are implicitly but sternly kept apart from us, and there they stay. The wall is invisible and intangible, but none the less effective.

Do the inhabitants of other quarters stroll through these projects, so close by, back to back with the towns from which they are separated? No, for they are thought perilous, often with good reason. But let's not forget that their inhabitants have already fallen (or been pushed) into the depths of that danger everyone fears, into permanent social exclusion, and such an absolute one as to become commonplace.

And do we often see the dwellers in the urban fringes wander anywhere but in their own parts of town, or in similar areas? What do they share with the rest of us, apart from television, an occasional journey on the subway, advertising and the employment agency? Do we see them anywhere but on television, shown in their own zoo in programmes of an ethnological or folklore nature, or alternatively during some rough raids in our own zoo, exactly as warriors making forays outside their own frontiers.

Who drew the lines of those frontiers? Do these young people really prefer their technical secondary schools to the grammar schools of the better parts of town? Would they rather live in their bleak surroundings than somewhere more privileged? Are they made of stuff that forbids them to want these things? Or is it just a question of their poverty?

One and one only social group linking them to a society obviously not their own is the police. And here the relationship is so close, one in which the frequently tragic interactions of both sides so exactly and predictably respond to each other, are so much a part of the same routine and the same brutalities, in the same trap, that their rituals often appear almost incestuous.

The one institutional decor organized almost exclusively for their benefit, in line with concepts tied to their future and appropriate for their fate is prison.

However, there is another ground where they meet the other side at close quarters: school. They are confronted there, directly, often for the first time – which will sometimes prove to be the last one – with those who exclude them. There they are face to face, on the same territory, in an intimate, everyday and officially compulsory relationship. And most of the time, it is at this very point that quite conspicuously they will fail to meet.

The main reason being that whatever their financial situation, social conditions or motivations, the teachers come from the privileged side of the wall and will leave their pupils on the other side.

Whatever their worth and their necessity, the teachers and the educational institution are connected to those who exclude, humiliate, and have consigned the parents (and thus their children) to dead-ends to forget them there, stranded outside life for their lifetime. The teachers seem to be somehow the delegates of a nation which in general treats such pupils and their families as untouchables, whether or not they are citizens of the country. Even if unjustly, this may feel like an enemy intrusion, the violation of territory usually left so abandoned.

However legitimate that incursion may be, as a last rem-
nant of fading promises, a last democratic effort, the last
indispensable sign of a sharing, of at least an intention for
equality, the last trace of a right whose worth, were it only
symbolic, is irreplaceable – it can seem like provocation
when experienced by children who are sacrificed in advance.
And whatever the attitudes and sentiments of the teachers,
that irruption is part of the continuum of general contempt
and takes place right on the terrain where that contempt is
writ large, right on the terrain that shows up its consequences.

Education? It could be the greatest gift ever to these
schoolchildren, a way of sharing the very best there is, an
authorized share of magic, but also a unique, ultimate recourse. However, they are offered the barest minimum of
that education, and it is interrupted as soon as possible. The
notion of a 'last chance' emphasizes their distress and the
peril threatening them and induces an insidious anxiety
which heightens tension in both teachers and pupils.

Nostalgia is also heightened for the values of the other
side, beckoning, tempting, but remaining as distant, out of
reach as ever, forbidden, while, contrary to appearances,
they are not even valid any more elsewhere. They are held
out to them much as Alice in her baleful Wonderland was
offered exquisite but fleeting food, whisked away before she
could help herself. The fake offer of what will never be
savoured suggests another metaphor: the turning of the knife
in the wound.

Must it not be thought a bad joke, an additional insult, to
teach children about the rudiments of a life already denied
to them, an already confiscated life, a life of which they are
deprived in advance (and a life no longer viable anyway)?

How are they to be convinced that education is a final
manifestation of republican ideals? A last hope even for the
society that is victimizing them? Yes, for that society too.
Mostly for that society! How is it possible to make them
understand that society is caught, as they are, in the tangles of
a net, in stories, fibs and fabrications that obscure its history?

But, after all, isn't that precisely what ought to be taught?

It so happens that regarding these 'stories' or this crucial moment of history (which is also a time when some want us to believe that history is at an end and that, as nothing is said about history any more, there is nothing to say about it), the children of these lost places are in the vanguard of our time. In fact, society today is regressive. These children are not. Society is blind to its own history, which organizes itself without it and eliminates it. These children are at the cusp of history. They have *already* been sidelined, and live not so much rejected by a society in decline while claiming that it will endure, as in advance of it. They probably represent samples of what is awaiting the majority of earth people if they do not wake up and take steps to organize themselves within a civilization recognized and admitted as different, uprooted, instead of agreeing to live mistreated, covered with shame, on the terms of a vanished age, instead of wasting away, spurned and passive, before maybe perishing and thus ridding the champions of a new era of their superfluous presence.

These children, these precursors – no one has even taken the trouble of trying to put them off or cheat them so that the least of these excluded children, by the very fact of being etched in what has to be called our modernity, by the very fact of experiencing it in the raw, and of not accepting it, resigned as adults are – these children can sense what most people elsewhere don't know or ignore.

How could they not instinctively sense the absurdity of attempts to condition them to a programme which excludes them? An imperturbable programme given as exemplary and attempting to fit within the damage that is not taken into account and that derives from it. A programme in which social exclusion is not mentioned, and where there is no thought of remedying it; but rather to justify it or at least consent to it. A programme created by and for a society which to a great extent seems to consider the social exclusion of this youth and their own people as logical, desirable and even insufficient. A programme in which these young people are supposed to belong but can have the impression of being tacitly reserved for the role of pariahs.

Is it really encouraging for them to see people from the same zone (the social classes today are thought of in terms of zones), people close to them, sometimes their very families, often their neighbours, expelled by charter plane, or threatened to be so, and outcast by an entire society still unable to see that it is becoming 'globally' superfluous itself, and implicitly undesirable?

For it is possible to be an emigrant *on the spot*; poverty can make you an exile in your own land. But official exclusions have a definite virtue: they persuade those who are spared that they are socially included. A fictitious status to which they cling.

What the youth of these areas seem to sense is that their education is handed down by people who have been cheated themselves and are in a difficult position. All in all, this education is a perverted one since it holds out prospects that are and will all remain closed to them and, even worse perhaps, are closed and will be closed to the teachers themselves.

And again that subject is not on the curriculum.

Nor is the coarseness of those squalid ghettos of destitution of the United States, or the teeming slums of Manila, the *favelas* of Rio, and so many other such places. That geography is ignored as well as the infernal lists of the starving in Africa, South America and elsewhere. Lists of these misfortunes that each time are undergone by a conscious being who was not created to starve and be bullied even if that became his fate. None the less, it should be understood that all these millions of scandals are experienced one by one, that each time they devour an entire, unique life, that same precious, indecipherable entity that develops and perishes in every one of us from the cradle to the grave.

We may not 'acknowledge' this horror scattered on other bodies than ours, bodies that are synchronous to us, but we 'know' about it. And we know that it is also experienced among us, at our gates, less brutal than on other continents but probably a lonelier, a more humiliating experience, because public opinion turns on it and accuses it, for the very reason that it is not everyone's lot here. Hence the experience is even more despised and the people going through it are even more wounded by the nation that 'shelters' them and does it so badly.

Maybe it is left to the children of the excluded, the excluded children, to teach us that we know all that.

Indeed, in theory, their schooling represents a weapon against excess and injustice, a last resort against rejection. But how are schoolchildren to assimilate that? Have they been given the means of doing so? Or some clues? Moreover, for schoolchildren of all ages and all circles, access to knowledge has an austere, often off-putting aspect; it calls for efforts worth making to learn how to be part of a society – but what about learning how to be rejected by it?

Of that society held up as a model by the education deriving from it, these youngsters know the backstages, not of power, but those of its results. They are familiar with what is usually secret and concealed. Through all the disorder and shortcomings of their daily lives, don't they subconsciously detect the irreversible rifts that precede collapse?

They are discarded by the roadside, but there is less and less traffic going down the road itself, while more and more of the other inhabitants of the planet, of all classes and expectations, join them and wind up with them.

The road no longer leads to the same places. Where does it lead to? No one knows. Those who might know, the promoters behind the new civilization, are not on it either. They live and move around elsewhere, taking very little interest in the old landscape. To them, it is already part of a past destined for oblivion or folklore.

Instinctively, no doubt the children guess that teaching or pretending to teach what is cruelly anachronistic as if it is still relevant is one of the only ways – the best one – for deceiving oneself so as to go on living by criteria now invalid, and thus ratifying them and prolonging illusions that engender fatal misunderstandings and sterile suffering.

Here we return to the widespread fraud that imposes the phantom systems of a vanished society on us, presenting the extinction of work as a mere temporary eclipse. What good is it, then, to go on dwelling on the problems of the poor suburbs? They represent only the extreme symptoms of what is happening at every level of our societies, although with rhythms and modes somewhat different, and made different. Everywhere are felt the divergence, the gap, the distance between the recommended, codified world offered by education, and the world it aims at, where it is taught but where it no longer manages to preserve its meaning. To preserve any meaning.

The diversity and content of the curriculum is not at issue here; on the contrary. Since the path leading to employment is closing, education might at least aim at offering these transitional generations a culture which would give their presence in the world, their simple human presence, a meaning, allowing them a glimpse of the possibilities open to human beings, an opening onto the fields of human knowledge, and therefore offering them reasons for living, paths to take, directions for the immanent dynamism.

Yet rather than preparing new generations for a way of life which would not have to involve employment any more (now practically inaccessible), they are being forced into closed-off places that refuse them, converting them as a result into outcasts excluded from what does not even exist. Into unfortunates.

Under the pretext of looking to a future that was accessible only in a bygone context, we persist in neglecting and rejecting what was not devoted to it in the programme, while preserving what we imagine is necessary to attain an already vanished future. Because the future as foreseen is not unfolding, we envisage no other future than to be deprived of it. Because these young people have nothing, everything is taken away from them, beginning with what seems to be gratuitous, a useless luxury, and what belongs to culture, that is what remains in the human domain, the only one for which these groups, in incommensurable numbers and banished from the economic world, still have a calling for.

The tendency, on the contrary, is to consider that they are not prepared enough – and not directly enough – to join the firms which do not want them, to which they are no longer necessary, but yet for which, and for nothing else, they are supposed to be trained. We are, or believe we should be, obsessed with going for what is supposed to be the most realistic and is in fact the most dreamt, fictitious. We set our sights on a single goal, reproaching ourselves with not holding to it enough: the idea being to launch pupils into a now non-existent wage-earning world as early as possible. It is thought any school subjects, any track which would not seem suitable for catapulting schoolchildren straight into jobs should be pruned away. The advice is to aim more and more exclusively for on-the-job training directly as a way of finding the work which of course fails to materialize. This is called being 'concrete'.

As for frivolous knick-knacks that lead nowhere, contempt is poured on such incongruous fancies! Some young people, those from the right side of the tracks, will become initiated in thinking; they will be called upon to understand and admire the artistic, literary, scientific and other achievements of those who come into the perfectly acceptable category of cultural 'suppliers' to their families. A few of them will even join such somewhat irresponsible yet socially respectable groups – and sometimes proving to be flattering company. Not to say in small doses – even profitable. Isn't there a market for their wares?

However, some dreaming souls will very wisely remark, since these things are superfluous should they really be taught to people who are no use? Is there really any economic sense in it? Why give such people the means of waking up to the reality of their situation? They will only suffer more from it and start criticizing it, whereas now they are keeping so quiet. Better to get them more deeply involved and further entrenched in the condition of 'job-seekers', an occupation which will keep them good as gold for quite some time. 'Set aside', is one of Van Gogh's expressions, one that shows he had understood it all. 'It is better that I be as not being.' These young people could profit by his example.

In order to 'be' (or to be as 'not being') – since not everyone can become a painter, still less a painter like Van Gogh – many of them become hooligans, delinquents, and it will be one more proof of their wicked natures.

And incidentally, since they are there all the same, why not profit from the situation to obtain the few apprentices and employees who are still sometimes required and get them ready, trained at the taxpayer's expense, delivered for immediate use? It would be silly not to take advantage of them. No sooner said than done. An outstanding initiative! The CES,[21] the CIE,[22] tax exemptions, the subsidies pour down among other delicate attentions favouring 'big' businesses, enabling them to extend their benefits and let their love for their neighbour shine more brightly.

[21] Contrat d'emploi solidarité, aimed at the non-competitive sector. The worker gets a half-time job, paid on the minimum wage.
[22] Contrat d'initiative emploi, aimed at the long-term unemployed. A company gets a monthly grant and a reduction in labour costs when it hires one of these.

VIII

Our systems, they say, are meant to repose to a great extent on the decision-makers' irrepressible love for their supposed neighbours, or failing that for their fellow creatures. They therefore urge companies to call themselves 'citizens', and once proclaimed 'a citizen company' to appear really civic-minded. They do not compel the company; they invite it, so sure they are of its good instincts. Thus sought out, how could one envisage for even a second that, once forewarned of what is good and what is bad, the company doesn't opt for the good?

In passing, let's pay tribute to the idea of the 'citizen company'. No surrealist would have dared to invent it!

However, once a 'citizen', or invited to become one, and once supposedly leaning towards the good, the company finds itself offered tons of subsidies, tax exemptions and chances of advantageous contracts if it will recruit workers and refrain from relocating. It is kind enough to accept the subsidies but does not hire workers, does relocate, or threatens to do so if everything doesn't go to its liking. Unemployment rises. Everything starts all over again.

But what on earth made so many countries and political parties, and first of all left-wing parties, believe for years that prosperity in business means that of society, or that growth creates jobs? And they still believe it, or try to, and at least claim they do. In 1980, I wrote: 'The workers' parties demand state financing for private firms, which will thus be able to go on exploiting them in the best interest of their profits, and will in turn create jobs or unemployment in accordance with the vagaries of the day, stock exchange rates, the air of crisis and crisis in the air.'[23]

It was always predictable that 'business incentives' would not create jobs, or at least not to the prophesied extent – far from it. Ten or fifteen years ago, developing that would have taken guts; there were very few clues. Today it has become obvious. None the less the system is still being implemented.

No one seems to ask by what miraculous operation the destitution due to unemployment results in the granting of favours, without any result, to companies that bewail their poverty when the economic world is doing very well, and still better for being courted, pampered to no avail, that is thought capable of that benevolent kindness expected from it in vain, and that would consist in having the amiability to hire workers with the credits generously granted for that purpose, whereas unemployment thrives.[24]

But why encumber companies with a moral burden that they are not cut out for? It's up to the political powers to make them do so. A mere request will bring no results, except some theatrical effects intended to provide the public with a very vague pledge. Governments whispering timid suggestions are not unaware that if those companies responded positively they would be traitors to their own interests, which are all their *raison d'être* and the basis of their ethics.

But above all, why not face this reality? Companies do not hire workers for the excellent reason that they do not need them. It is this situation that has to be faced, and it is nothing short of a metamorphosis. What could be more impressive,

---

[23] *La Violence du calme.*

[24] In 1958, France had 25,000 unemployed. In 1996, the number had risen to nearly 3.5 million. This is by no means a French privilege. It is an international phenomenon. There are about 120 million unemployed world-wide, including some 35 million in the industrialized countries: 18 million in Europe (Martine Hassoun and Frédéric Rey, *Les Coulisses de l'emploi*, Paris: Arléa, 1995).

more terrifying? And calling for a superhuman degree of imagination? Who is going to have the courage and talent to do so?

Meanwhile, the companies that benefit from the situation go on downsizing, in large numbers, which is now regarded as commonplace. 'Restructuring' abounds, a word that sounds vigorous and constructive, but it includes mainly these 'social plans' which really means programmed redundancies that today cement the economy. What then is the point of being shocked that they in fact destructure whole lives and families, and invalidate all political and economic wisdom? Should all these hypocritical, wicked words be denounced? Should a dictionary of those words be published?

Once again: the vocation of business has nothing to do with being charitable. What is perverse is presenting business as 'a dynamic force' acting in obedience to moral and social imperatives relating to the general good. While indeed they do have a duty and an ethic, but it orders them to make profits, which in itself is quite licit, legally spotless. Yes. But today, rightly or wrongly, employment represents a negative factor, prohibitively expensive, useless and detrimental to profit. Harmful.

Yet 'creating wealth' is still held up to us as the only factor able to mobilize business decision-makers, who are presented as the only ones able to create growth, thanks to the wealth they create. A growth that would immediately result in jobs. As if it were possible to ignore the fact that if in other times when work was indispensable, situations of growth opened the way to a thriving labour market, it is no longer the case now that work has become superfluous.

Employment, so fervently hymned and invoked, the subject of so many incantations, is regarded by those who could provide it as nothing but an archaic and practically useless factor, a source of financial deficit. Pruning jobs has become one of the most fashionable management methods, one of the most efficient of adjustment variables, the favourite way of saving money and an essential agent of profit.

When will this be taken into account – not to wax indignant or oppose it, but to detect its logic? And since both the ability and the will to fight it are lacking, we could at least cease being duped and playing into the hands of a political propaganda that lulls us with its never disinterested promises, or of those economic interests that will get more advantages from such situations as long as they are not examined. We might then find other ways and turn aside from those dangerous paths we are directed towards and that indeed we insist on taking.

How long will those who are awake pretend to be asleep?

When, for instance, will we see that 'wealth' is no longer 'created' by 'creating' material goods so much as by wholly abstract speculations, with no links (or only quite loose ones) to productive investments? To a great extent, the 'wealth' on display represents a vague entity, serving as an excuse for the deployment of derivatives which bear little relation to it.

Derivatives, which are now invading the economy, reduce it to casino games or bookmakers' practices. The derivatives markets are bigger today than the traditional ones. Now this new form of economy no longer invests: it bets. Its activities are in the nature of bets, but ones with no real stakes and that do not rely so much on material values or even on more symbolic financial exchanges (which are at least initially based, albeit distantly, on real assets) as on virtual assets invented for the sole purpose of playing their own games. This speculative economy consists of betting on the variations of business which does not yet exist, and maybe never will. And from there, in relation to those virtual variations, playing around with bets on securities, debts, interest and exchange rates, now skewed of any sense, connected with purely arbitrary projections, approaching the wildest fantasy or prophesies of a parapsychological nature. It consists, above all, in betting on the result of all these bets. And then on the results of the bets made on the results of those bets, and so on.

A whole traffic where what does not exist is bought and sold, where neither real assets nor even symbols based on these assets are traded but where one buys and sells, for example, the risks taken by medium- or long-term contracts that are still to be concluded or that are merely imagined, where debts too are sold and will then again be negotiated, resold, rebought endlessly; where most often by mutual agreement contracts are settled that trade in wind, on virtual values that are not yet created but already guaranteed, that produce other contracts, always concluded by mutual agreement, involving the negotiation of these very contracts! The market in risks and debts allows dealers to indulge in these small follies in all fake security.

Such guarantees over virtual assets or values are endlessly negotiated, and further trafficking is conducted around those negotiations. So many imaginary transactions, speculations with no other object or subject but themselves, make up an immense, artificial, acrobatic market based on nothing but itself, remote from any reality but its own, a closed, fictitious and imaginary one, endlessly complicated by unbridled hypotheses from which extrapolations are made. Speculators endlessly and *ad infinitum* speculate on speculation. And on the speculation over speculations. This is a flimsy, illusory market based on and firmly rooted in simulacra, a market hallucinated to such an extent as to become poetic.

'Options over options over options', former Chancellor Helmut Schmidt ironically commented on Arte[25] the other night,[26] yet seeming slightly alarmed, as by unruly children. He confirmed the fact that 'a hundred times more deals' are made on these surrealistic markets than on any others.

Hence the famous free market economy, regarded as fundamental, serious, and responsible for populations, as a power unto itself – as *the* power – is under control, caught up in the fever – one could say the hard drug – of tractations, of manipulations around its own trafficking which result in gigantic, rapid, brutal gains. They seem almost secondary to the intoxication of dealing, the maniacal pleasure and the demented sense of power they induce.

[25] French–German television channel
[26] 8 April 1996.

This is the meaning 'wealth creation' is taking on. It becomes a distant, increasingly evanescent pretext, also superfluous, for these obsessive operations – a St Vitus's dance upon which the planet itself and all our lives increasingly depend.

Such markets do not lead to any creation of wealth or real production. They do not even need real estate. They employ hardly any staff, since a few telephones and computers are all that is needed, when the chips are down, to handle virtual deals. Yet it is on such markets which don't involve the labour of other people and aren't producing real goods that companies (among others) are more and more often investing more and more of their profit shares since profit can be made there in a bigger and quicker way than elsewhere. Thus subsidies and advantages that are granted for these companies to hire more and more often end up in such infinitely more profitable neo-finance-hedge-betting games!

In this context, job creation from 'wealth creation' would come close to humanitarianism, since growth (in fact or profit alone) does not lead to the development or even the exploitation of earthly products but to this strange, oneiric way of marking time and certainly not – not any more – to the development of human labour, or *a fortiori* a larger workforce. Instead, it often represents an opportunity of setting up or perfecting technological systems based on robotization and able to reduce human potential, hence to save on labour costs.

It is common knowledge that booming, profitable companies slash the workforce. According to the experts, nothing is more advantageous. All the more so as they are still awarded job-creation premiums without having to be accountable or being compelled to recruit with the aid provided for such a purpose. It is barely insinuated to them (could you believe successfully?) that they should not use these grants to more profitable ends. What would you guess they choose to do?

Here one finds oneself toying with guilty thoughts: what if growth, far from creating jobs, rather created their elimination, from which that growth often stemmed? Actually, doesn't the flagrant ineptitude in the management of social economy allow a more rational management of financial markets?

Recently one could read in the press that 'Persuading companies to participate in the "national employment drive" is one thing, but discouraging their restructuring plans is another. *Although they benefited greatly in 1995*,[27] such leading industrial companies as Renault, IBM, GEC-Alsthom, Total and Danone have planned considerable staffing reductions for 1996 . . . Not to mention all the downsizing put on ice.' Which trade union or left-wing paper published these subversive comments? As a matter of fact, *Paris Match*[28] did.

At the end of the 1970s and during the 1980s – and it is still going on – business was so holy that any sacrifices were worth making to preserve it or see it thrive even more. The business community explained in a scholarly way that it was to avoid unemployment that they had to practise slashing. Thus how could they not be warmly encouraged to do so?

Above all, one must face up to one's responsibilities. Downsizing, economizing on labour costs is one of the most effective of cost-saving devices. How many politicians and managing directors swear they are going to create employment and boast they are cutting jobs all within the very same speech?

The non-work of the non-waged in fact represents a capital gain for business, thus a contribution to 'wealth creation', a profit in a way for those who do not employ them, and even more so for those who don't employ them any more. Wouldn't it be fair for a share of the profit generated by their absence, a share in the interest earned by not employing them to go to them?

However, aren't those savings on labour costs supposed to lead to increased opportunities for favouring some of the inevitable 'wealth creation' so famous for producing and providing jobs? To point out that the wealth thus created has

---

[27] Author's italics.
[28] 21 March 1996.

no effect other than increasing some fortunes would indeed sound petty. While the decision-makers and company directors are so generous! Let's take a lesson from them and listen to one of them speaking on the radio:[29] according to him, companies have a mission which must be given a meaning, and it will, he tells us, be a 'human meaning'. Not surprising at all as, so he confirms, companies are 'citizen companies'; their one and only law is 'civism'. They are fighting an economic war, and it is a war for employment. Nevertheless, he notes that 'A company can share only the wealth it produces.' Here the audience can't help telling itself that it can also not share it. Our humanitarian none the less observes that 'the profitability logic must never be forgotten.' As for 'recruiting for the sake of recruiting'? He suddenly sounds perplexed and quite doubtful. He decides: 'Only when growth allows recruitment', but doesn't say what degree of growth will authorize this valorous gesture. He suddenly sounds more cheerful, much more in his element and speaks of 'finding markets, increasing productivity'. He gets so lively that he gives a recipe: 'Alleviate the burden on industry.' His voice now sounds buoyant, he is loquacious, he positively chants: 'Cutting costs per hour . . . reductions in employers' social security contributions and in welfare costs . . .'

Another example, also from the airwaves,[30] comes from the chairman of the CNPF (the National Council of French Business Leaders), the boss of bosses: speaking of the benefits recently awarded again to his troops (or rather, enthusiastically offered to them) so that they would hire workers, he seems reticent – not about accepting them, as he and his flock are preparing to do, but about what is asked in return (or rather, timidly suggested). Outraged, he finally allows that so and so in such a firm might *perhaps*, thanks to the subsidies granted to him, 'try to bring about a slight reduction in the annual rate of redundancy, now standing at 5 per

[29] France-Culture (August 1996), interview with J. Bousquet by D. Jamet.
[30] On Radio Luxemburg, 8 July 1995.

cent'. But to speak of a trade-off in this context 'shows an imperfect understanding of economic reality'.[31] He rather suggests 'reducing public expenditure instead of taxing business that creates employment'. He thinks it is 'not for the law courts to concern themselves with redundancies . . . As for recycling, we must do as we see fit.' He ends by admitting that there are 'political moments when it is inopportune to lay off', although 'streamlining is necessary if we are to adapt to the world situation.' One might have guessed it.

However, such altruistic impulses are supervised by world organizations as the World Bank, the OECD and the IMF, among others, and are even determined and regulated by them. These organizations rule the planetary economy, that is to say, the political life of the nations, in harmony with the private economic powers, which are really in league rather than competing with each other!

While nations and their politicians seem so sorry about unemployment, and proclaim themselves fervently mobilized against it, obsessed by it night and day, the OECD has published a rather more subtle opinion in a report,[32] claiming that 'to obtain a given adjustment of labour costs, a higher level of conjunctural unemployment will be necessary.'

Always with the same fraternal and cheerful eloquence – much as advice to the lovelorn might give the recipe for how to attract and keep the man or woman of one's dreams: 'the eagerness of the workforce to accept low-paid jobs depends partly on the relative generosity of unemployment benefits. . . . All countries should reduce the period of benefit payments when it is too long, or tighten up the conditions in which benefit is granted.'[33] This is telling them.

---

[31] *Tribune Desfosse*, 30 May 1994.

[32] OECD, *Jobs Study* (Paris, June 1994), quoted by Serge Halimi in 'Les Chantiers de la démolition sociale', *Le Monde diplomatique* (July 1994).

[33] World Bank, *World Department Report: Workers in an Integrating World* (Oxford: Oxford University Press, 1995), quoted by Jacques Decornoy in 'Travail, capital . . . pour qui chantent les lendemains', *Le Monde diplomatique* (September 1995).

The private, international, multinational or transnational powers don't burden themselves with the desire to please, that dread of political powers. There's no turning on the charm here; no making eyes at the electorate. No idle chatter or qualms here; no making up. The game is played in full view, among one another. The aim is to get to the essential: how to manage the profit? How to bring profit about? How can world enterprise work for the benefit of all big business leaders united?

The World Bank comes straight to the point, without fuss or circumlocution, stating: 'An increased flexibility of the labour market – despite its bad reputation, the word being a euphemism for wage cuts and redundancies – is essential in all areas where thorough reforms are being carried out.' The IMF goes further: 'The European governments must not allow fears of the consequences brought about by the effects of their action on the distribution of revenue to prevent them from throwing themselves boldly into fundamental reform of the labour markets; their easing up will be achieved by overhauling unemployment benefit systems, the guaranteed minimum wage and the measures protecting employment.'[34]

The battle is brewing against the excluded. They really take up too much space. As has been pointed out above, they are not nearly excluded enough. They are a drag.

However, the OECD knows how to deal with those who do not work unless kicked in the ass by destitution. Its report on employment and the recommended 'strategies' for obtaining the workers' 'eagerness' is, as we have seen, most explicit. Moreover, 'the productivity of many new jobs is low and such jobs are viable only with very low wages to match.'[35] But as that plays on a much wider range of jobs, 'a large proportion of wage-earners will remain unemployed unless the labour markets are made more flexible, particularly in Europe.' QED!

---

[34] IMF, *Bulletin*, 23 May 1994, quoted by Halimi, 'Les Chantiers'.
[35] OECD, *Jobs Study* (June 1994), quoted ibid.

In other words, employers (who are not supposed, in truth, to show social concern) will agree to making a few listless efforts to hire or refrain from sacking workers only if those workers are conditioned to accept anything. Which is the least they can do: given the state into which they are have already been reduced, and the state they are threatened with, they are in no condition to be choosy.

So that it is quite understandable to dispose of these idlers and to discuss them without their having access to those discussions, and also understandable that those who still retain dignity speak instead of them, and plan training them as they would animals, using such efficient ways as integrating them for their own good in a methodically devised and deliberately organized 'insecurity', with such painful fall-out that it can ruin lives and sometimes even cut them short.

Isn't being concerned with them an act of charity?

But what else is ever done? Every moment, every action is devoted to them. There is nothing in the world-wide, internationalized, globalized, deregularized, deregulated, relocated, flexible and transnational system that does not act to their detriment, nothing that does not militate against them.

If only through that strange mania for consigning populations, at any price, to non-existent jobs in a society which clearly no longer needs them, and for refusing to seek paths other than those, so obviously closed off and defunct, that still claim to lead to those jobs, and are devastating.

Also through this mania of clinging to adversity arising from the 'economic horrors' evoked by Rimbaud, making them out a natural phenomenon older than time.

Here is a description of the situation in the United States given by Edmund S. Phelps,[36] a noted economist, author and professor at Columbia University, a moderate who dispassionately analyses the advantages and drawbacks of an array of economic reactions to unemployment. First, there are the beneficial effects of restructuration which, thanks to 'the insecurity thus affecting the workers, allows employers to

[36] *Le Monde*, 12 March 1996.

reduce payroll expenditure and create jobs especially in the services sector, [which are] not only poorly paid but precarious'.

Still described by Mr Phelps, here is the ideal man of whom the OECD dreams: 'The American wage-earner who loses his job absolutely has to find another one as soon as possible. Unemployment benefits represent only a very small part of his previous salary, and they will be granted for a maximum of six months. They will not be complemented by any social benefits (for housing, education, etc.) In short, he will find himself stripped naked, living on his own resources.' (And what, one wonders, might those be?) 'He must find and accept a job very soon, even if it does not correspond to what he is looking for.' The trouble is that 'it is often difficult for these unskilled workers to find a job, even a very low-paid one.'

What Mr Phelps chiefly deplores is that 'the unemployed then take up other activities: they beg, deal drugs, get involved in street trafficking. Criminality rises. In a way they have created their own welfare state through these networks.' This clearly makes for a messy situation, and prevents Mr Phelps from condemning the European system of welfare benefits that has, in his view, the advantage of avoiding the degree of delinquency its absence in the United States creates, its drawback being that it tends 'to reduce incentives to find a job'.

Here we are again. Yet Mr Phelps is not unaware (and the American wage-earner, 'stripped naked' and provided with 'incentives' might have something to say here) that there is not a plethora of jobs; there are not masses of them, and the worst destitution, the fiercest quest are not enough to find work even if only for a quarter of an hour. He knows that unemployment is endemic and permanent. He knows that 'incentives' for finding a job nearly always mean that no job will be found: that the desperate, despairing search in which innumerable unemployed people engage, with all the financial cost it entails in stamps, telephone calls and travelling, usually fails even to elicit a reply. Besides, given the demographic evolution, establishing or re-establishing a decent situation on this planet would mean creating a billion new jobs in the next ten years, at a time when work is disappearing! Mr Phelps must know that the problem is not to provide the unemployed with incentives for seeking jobs, but to enable them to find some, since that is the only pattern that will allow their survival. Has he thought of an alternative: changing that pattern?

Above all, he knows that there is no shortage of job-seekers but only of jobs.

Seeking employment must surely come close to an act of piety, for as far as we know, the search for jobs does not create them. Otherwise, with all those who have been provided with 'incentives' and who try hard to find jobs, with all who dream of a job as if it were the Holy Grail during their vain searching, it would have become common knowledge. And with all those who accept these almost always precarious lesser evils, thus allowing them to resume so recommendable a search – all those casual jobs, part-time, temporary work, training periods, phoney training schemes and other ersatz work where they are so often exploited; with all those who collapse having found none, if the supply were an 'incentive' to the creation of jobs, we would certainly have heard of it.

However, is it really to seek 'unfindable' jobs that one is 'incited'? Is that the real stake? Wouldn't it be instead to obtain the small amount of work still needed to be done at an even lower price, as near as possible to nothing? And thus to increase insatiable profits? Or incidentally to emphasize the guilt of victims who are never assiduous enough in begging for what is refused to them, and does not exist anyway.

It would be about time! Gary Becker,[37] winner of the Nobel Prize for Economics, admonishes us indignantly, while deploring 'the generous nature of the welfare benefits' disbursed by 'certain European governments', which have,

[37] *Le Monde*, 28 March 1996.

like France, 'extravagantly raised the minimum wage of 37 francs [= £3.70; $6.27] an hour'. He diagnoses 'a serious illness', not without warning us that 'when work is expensive and lay-offs hard to carry out, companies are reluctant to replace those workers who *leave*[38] them.' Some surprise. What a pity that Mr Becker never had a chance to meet Nanny Beppa: no doubt they would have exchanged fruitful remarks about geese who lay golden eggs!

To tell the truth, it isn't incentives to look for jobs that are at issue but incentives to accept being exploited and to consider oneself ready to do anything rather than perish of destitution or cease to be excluded ... but excluded for having been definitively rejected by life.

The aim is also to weaken, to crush morally and physically too those who might otherwise become a danger to 'social cohesion'. Above all, it is to condition for the worst – in advance – the populations who have to face it. Precisely so that they won't then confront it but submit to it, already anaesthetized.

As for profit, so determinant a factor, no mention has been made of it, as usual, just as it is usual to invert the question and claim to be interested solely in the fate of those who in fact are always being pressured and whose only hope is to pray for that situation to go on: as pressurable entities they are still tolerated. Otherwise ...

But let us set our minds at rest: they still are pressurable. Let's remember how Mr Phelps, a moderate, showed that if people sought employment, inaccessible as it has become, at any price, and that if at the same time, in addition to a lack of resources, in addition to the loss or threatened loss of a roof, in addition to the time spent in being thrown out, in addition to the contempt of others and of self-deprecation, in addition to the vacuity of a terrifying future, in addition to physical deterioration due to penury and anguish, in addition

---

[38] Author's italics. The euphemism will be appreciated. The Beckerian line of argument is particularly baffling when he says that 'taxes, like death, are inevitable.' Better leave the interpretation of this curious assertion to psychoanalysis.

to the damage done to couples and families often broken up, in addition to despair – if in addition to all that they find themselves simultaneously driven back into even more 'insecurity' – a technically predictable one this time – and without assistance or, at the best, with assistance calculated to be insufficient, at least more so than before, then they will be ready to accept, to endure or suffer any form of employment, at any price, in any conditions – and even to find none.

Yet the sole reason that could 'incite' its possessors to provide what little work they still have at their disposal lies in their possibility of exchanging it at the low rates accepted by the unfortunate souls entrapped in 'insecurity'. Job creation? Perhaps. But insecurity must be created first! And it's even better to fetch that insecurity where it is, on certain continents.

Of course, among the masses whose social insecurity has been planned in cold blood, only a meagre percentage of individuals will benefit from the low-paid jobs which will hardly get them out of destitution. For the other ones nothing will remain but insecurity, with its train of humiliations, privations and dangers. Also with the abbreviation of some lives.

But at least profit will have made profit.

IX

In some parts of the planet 'incentives' to work are in full swing. Penury and the absence of any social welfare system reduce the cost of labour and of work to practically nothing: a true paradise for businesses, a dream of an assembly line to which is added that of tax havens. Many corporations do not hesitate to make a beeline for such places.

Hence those relocations of firms that wreak such havoc, brutally withdrawing jobs from inhabitants of whole areas, sometimes ruining whole regions, impoverishing the nation itself. Once the firm has gone to other climes, it will no longer pay taxes in its old locations, and it will be for the state and local authorities, left high and dry, to finance the unemployment created by the firm – that is, to finance the choices it has made for its own profit and to their detriment. Long-drawn-out financial support will be needed, since it is out of the question for the now unemployed workers, sacked so arbitrarily, to find new work in the geographical and professional sectors thus stricken and it will often be difficult for them ever to find any. As for capital flight from all tax circuits, it will deprive the swindled state's economic and social structures of resources.

But who, other than certain specialists, will feel any real indignation? Public opinion is far more concerned (and vehemently so) with the presence of 'foreigners' – that is to say, poor foreigners – who are assumed to be grabbing non-existent jobs, swindling native-born workers out of them and scrounging social welfare.

Down with immigrants coming in, good luck to capital going out! It is easier to take it out on the weak who are arriving, or are already there, or who even arrived long ago, than on the mighty who are deserting.

Let's not forget that if these immigrants emigrate to more prosperous countries, these same countries, including ours, have gone to their countries, and still do; and not only because of low wages. But to exploit their raw materials and natural resources, when they have not already used them up. Not to give away or distribute wealth is one thing; but to swipe the goods and deprive those areas of their advantages, lay claim to them on the pretext of being better qualified to exploit them (to the benefit of other regions) is another.

✓'Big' business linked to our governments is still economically colonizing many of these countries that have helped to enrich them. The already poor and now further impoverished inhabitants of countries whose resources have been 'borrowed', thus disrupting their specific economic ways of life – which are then no longer viable – therefore emigrate to the lands of those (now indignant) who descended on them first – in Africa, for instance – as visitors to their countries much more self-interested than our immigrants will ever be. But the truth is that all this goes on at levels neglected by the public at large.

Authorities and powers are careful not to throw light on anything. They fuel rejections, appreciate the vagueness in which relocation, capital flight and other more or less licit operations are hatched, and savour the tranquillity of their reign over their divided flock.

Thus do Western countries jealously close their terrestrial borders against the misery of the world, but allow the wealth to flee by virtual paths, the wealth to which their powerless and ill-informed citizens imagine they still have a right, which they believe they still own and have to defend, but which they let escape without emotion.

Those who are a drain on the already endangered payroll

are not the immigrants, but rather among the inhabitants of underdeveloped countries, those who have *not* gone abroad, who have *not* emigrated, but have remained in their own countries working for what can only be described as a pittance, without any social welfare, in conditions forgotten here. A manna to the multinationals, these people are held up as models, given as so many examples to which populations in more privileged countries should align themselves or, at least strive for, if they hope for another chance to join the livestock entitled to jobs – as long as some jobs remain.

Such opportunities and distribution are watched over by major world organizations like the World Bank, which considers that 'taxing the multinationals in order to prevent the migration of low-paid jobs to developing countries would be counter-productive',[39] or that 'the transfer of production abroad is an efficient strategy *for increasing the company's, market share in a competitive world*, or for minimizing its losses.'[40]

Markets can choose their poor from an enlarged area; the catalogue gets richer, for there are now the poor poor and the rich poor. And there are – they can always be found – even poorer poor, less difficult and 'demanding'. In fact, not demanding at all. Fantastic cut-price sales! Special offers everywhere. Work is available for nothing if you're willing to travel. A further advantage: choosing these poor – the poor poor – will make the rich poor poorer, and, once poorer, nearly as poor as the poor poor, they will in turn be less demanding. The great life!

The 'haves' are taking a strange revenge on the 'have-nots', the result of their dynamism, their greed and domination, but also of their spirit of enterprise. They contrive to turn everything to good account, transporting and reconstituting elsewhere the excesses of exploitations rendered null and void by history in the more industrialized countries and

[39] Quoted by Decornoy, 'Travail, capital'.
[40] Author's italics.

thought to have started disappearing almost everywhere, particularly after decolonization.

Not to mention the new technologies combined with the dramatic scarcity of jobs – for which they are largely responsible. The prompt perceptiveness of the private economy in seizing upon the prodigious capacities for ubiquity, synchronization and information offered by those technologies, in making use of short-circuit time and space, allows the international, multinational and transnational firms to flit about and flirt *à la* Don Juan gathering the choice nectar in whatever geographical sphere it pleases, rootless and fancy-free. It also allows the overwhelming spread of neo-colonialism.

Nothing could demonstrate the power and hegemony of the private economy better. Nothing, but for the indifference, the few reactions it arouses and their powerlessness when it does. Nothing but for the blackmail it exerts from then on on the policies of developed countries so as to make them fall into line, lower taxes, reduce public expenditure and social welfare systems, regulate deregulation and 'free' companies to lay off unimpeded, abolish the minimum wage, make work more flexible, and so on.

The result of such peremptory suggestions is to loosen the application of measures already much disputed and increasingly easy to avoid. Those suggestions or blackmail threats still encounter but weak resistance, public opinion that is jittery, rather despondent, easily distracted, and assiduously diverted toward a certain drowsiness.

It is true that populations are tired; they have given a lot already. They have thought a great deal. They are very much alone and feel crushed by the monstrous dimension of the one-track neo-liberal ideology. They are at a more dangerous turning point than it may seem, and that they prefer not to consider. For the time being, they are ready to listen to old legends trotted out during long evenings while they doze quietly, lulled by fairy-tales in which rich countries are always prosperous ones. Which is turning out – more and more – to be untrue.

Above all, we have experienced a revolution without having noticed it. A radical, mute revolution, without any stated theories or avowed ideologies; it came about in silence, by and through facts established without declaration, no comment, or any notification at all, facts noiselessly settled in history and in our settings. The very strength of that movement lies in the fact that it started being noticed only when already in place, and has been able in advance of its advent to prevent and paralyse any reaction against it.

Thus, the straitjacket of the markets has managed to sheathe us as tightly as a second skin, regarded as more fitting to us than that of our human body.

Thus, those days are gone when we deplored the underpayment of exploited labour in poverty-stricken countries often colonized by debt, among other things; what we are now deploring is the underemployment it causes in *our* countries, and are almost jealous of the unfortunate who in truth see their scandalous social conditions extended and confirmed – we are aware of it but there are no limits to our acquiescence.

It is usual, concerning employment, to deplore the fact that what is granted to some has been taken from others. Or to rejoice to see given to some what has been taken away from others. One could read for instance: 'At the Hôtel Matignon [the French prime ministerial offices], it is hoped that the objective of hiring young people for two out of every three vacancies will be achieved',[41] which is quite well meant, but means that out of three unemployed people, two older job-seekers will remain jobless, since the number of jobs available still does not increase, but, on the contrary, decreases most of the time. It's the same story when, while unemployment is rising, there is some satisfaction in seeing the percentage of the long-term unemployed fall; this time it is the young who will have found even fewer jobs than the rise in unemployment might have made them fear.

The fact is that the wrong problems are attacked and that

[41] *Paris Match*, 21 March 1966.

what is unmanageable is being claimed to be managed. Eliminating unemployment if only for one single individual is worth all the trouble that might be taken. But in the present state, the same cards can only be dealt out differently without putting anything right. There is no changing the direction of the slope; we can only go along with it, dealing with the real situation instead of a long-gone one.

Advice handed out individually to the unemployed by specialized organizations tells them how to be awarded an eventual, miraculously available job which, due to that fact, another jobless person won't get. Or rather, that numerous other jobless won't get, since there are so many applicants for any job at all, however deplorable it may be. (An example in France: the huge rush for CES (*Contrat Emploi Solidarité*) – part-time poorly paid jobs in the non-commercial sector that offer such brilliant careers and open the way, with luck, to another CES, a temporary, short-term contract. A part-time job. With pay equivalent to half the guaranteed minimum wage, about 2,800 francs a month.[42]) This advice, often the only advice given, offers nothing but helpful hints for being preferred and chosen rather than someone else. Since there is no tendency to an expansion of the overall payroll and the employment market, this has nothing to do with reducing the number of rejected applicants. Not even the surface of the problem has been scratched.

The galloping escalation in unemployment in the developed countries is tending, as we have seen, to make them attain, by insensible degrees, Third World poverty. We might have hoped to see the opposite occur and prosperity spread. Instead, it is poverty that is becoming 'globalized', making its way into previously privileged countries.

The decline – which is not that of the economy: the economy is flourishing! – emerges, less and less vague, accepted as a natural phenomenon, more and more managed by countries themselves more and more at the mercy of the

[42] 2800F in 1996 = $550; £350. [trans.]

private economy that, linked to the major world organizations we've already seen like the World Bank, the OECD, and the IMF, holds with them the mastery.

For the real regime under which we are living and whose authority keeps us under its influence with more and more power over us does not officially govern us but decides the configurations and substratum on which national governments will have to govern. It also decides on regulations, if not actual laws, that put the real decision-makers, transnational groups, and financial operators out of reach, protecting them from any control or constraint while they themselves constrain and control political power, divided up and distributed country by country – its distribution and demarcations ignored by the private economic forces, just as are frontiers.

Whatever its power, scope for action and capacity for responsibility, a government today operates within economic landscapes, networks and spheres of exploitation that determine its policies but are outside its province and don't depend on it, while it depends on them. Here is an almost anecdotal example: while all politicians shout themselves hoarse confiding their ardent commitment to the struggle against unemployment, the announcement of an actual fall in unemployment in the United States recently led to a slump in stock exchange rates throughout the world. *Le Monde* reported, on 12 March 1996:

> Friday 8 March will leave the mark of a black day on the financial markets. The publication of unexpectedly good employment figures in the USA had the effect of a cold shower – an apparent paradox to which the markets are accustomed. . . . The markets which mainly fear overheating and inflation were victims of real panic. . . . On Wall Street the Dow Jones index, which had already broken records on Tuesday, plummeted more than 3 per cent, the biggest percentage drop since 15 November 1991. European markets also fell steeply. . . . The financial markets seem particularly vulnerable to *any bad news*.[43] Analysts are awaiting

[43] Author's italics.

confirmation of the record figure of 705,000 jobs created in the USA in February, the highest since 1 September 1943. It was this statistic that set off the crisis. [The New York stock exchange] gave way to panic during the last two hours of trading on Friday. Wall Street may find itself in an environment that has become totally unfavourable, with a long-term rise in rates already well under way on one side, and on the other stagnation or even a fall in business profitability.

Another detail: the same market price soared some years ago when Xerox announced monstrous redundancies involving tens of thousands of workers. Now, the stock exchanges are hives of activity of that business world on which governments, if not nations rely.

Nevertheless, we still deplore in unison 'unemployment, the scourge of our time', and participate in electoral High Masses where prayers are said for the miraculous, guaranteed return of full-time employment. Statistical curves will tirelessly be published and tirelessly be discovered with shouts of distressed amazement and with a never discouraged sense of suspense, all of it to the greatest benefit of general submission and a more and more intense sense of gnawing panic that we can clearly see here has been once again *managed*.

Very discreetly managed, though! Did the drop in the stock exchange caused by the fall in unemployment strike public opinion? It was barely pointed out, as if it went without saying – 'just one of those things'. Was it taken as a sign or clue? Well, no, it didn't seem to be, even if the contradiction to the usual lyrical discourse and endless statements made by politicians and captains of industry was radical. Even if it amounted to a confession of the financial powers, thus admitting their true interests and therefore those of the political powers they influence – political powers that are navigating blind, steering by decisions taken elsewhere of which they are often ignorant. Even though it was a confession of governments, elected politicians and political candidates who, for electoral ends, and without much conviction, half-heartedly mimic for blasé audiences most unconvincing rescue drills supposed to find solutions for unemployment. The chief point of the exercise being to shore up the conviction that only grave but temporary and remediable setbacks in labour markets are in question within a society very logically organized around employment – even if around the lack of it.

Everyone pretends to believe in these rituals, the better to be convinced (although with more and more difficulty) that this is only a crisis period and not a mutation, not an already organized new mode of civilization whose logic assumes the ousting of employment, the extinction of salaried life and the marginalization of most human beings. And from then on . . . ?

Everyone clings to such rituals, so as to hear at least assurances that this is a passing phase of decline and not a new, dominant regime which will soon have no connection with any real system of exchange or any other support, for this kind of economy no longer belongs to anything but itself, is only directed towards itself. This probably being one of the very few utopias ever fulfilled, a unique example of anarchy in power (albeit purporting to stand for order), reigning over the world with more clout every day.

These are strange times, in which the proletariat, or rather the late proletariat, is struggling to recover its inhuman condition. While the Internationale, that old and somewhat corny old thing shelved among dusty props and forgotten refrains, seems to make a mute come-back, without words or music, silently intoned by the opposite camp. It unfolds as ambitious as ever yet less fragile, better armed and triumphant this time, for it has chosen the right means: those of potency rather than power.

X

From one 'Internationale' to the other, where is the 'final fight'? Won't any apparent conclusion see as always – and quite fortunately so – its consequences reappraised? *'Tout lasse, tout passe, tout casse'* ('Nothing lasts forever'), clever Nanny Beppa used to say, and everything proves her to have been right.

Nothing has ever been or ever will be definitive, even the most ossified situations. The twentieth century has made this obvious. And the question is not that of an 'end of history', as attempts have been made to make us believe. Instead, there is an unleashing of history, restless, in turmoil, manipulated and more determined than ever, more than ever turned towards one and only one meaning, a one-track way of thinking, orientated in one and only one direction: profit, whatever efficient camouflage may elegantly mask the fact.

In the face of it, what analyses, what protests or criticism, what opposition or even alternatives are there? None, if not the echo. With at most a few variations that might just be acoustic effects. Chiefly an upsurge of endemic deafness and blindness, while we are caught within vertiginous accelerations, in a flight towards a desertic conception of the world all the more disguised as we refuse to perceive it.

We are living in major historical times. It puts us at risk, at the mercy of a despotic economy whose powers and scope should at least be located, analysed and decoded. Globalized as it may be, committed to its power as the world may be, it remains to be understood, at least to be decided what place human life is still able to take in that outline. It is imperative at least to glimpse what we are involved in, to detect what we are still able to do, and how far encroachment, despoilment and conquest may yet go.

And if that conquest is approved on all sides, or at least ratified as inevitable by all parties – even if some may suggest the possibility of a few minor alterations, not to say a few reforms – isn't it at least possible for everyone to acquire at least the freedom to situate themselves lucidly, with a certain dignity, a certain autonomy, even when rejected?

Our blindness even to obvious clues has been going on for so long. New technologies, automation for instance, were predictable (and seemed to be so as so many promises) and weren't taken into account until the day businesses used them, and once having used them pragmatically at first, incorporated them without having given it much thought, until thanks to their technological advance, they in fact appropriated them and organized themselves around them to our detriment.

It could have been very different if, as of 1948, political thinkers had read the early works of Norbert Wiener[44] (not only the inventor of cybernetics but a very clear-sighted prophet of its consequences), and if they had been clever enough to deal with them, noting their long-term implications of wild hope and danger.

Extinction of work, technological power, the consequent metamorphoses, were all perceptible as well as an entirely different distribution of energy and other definitions of space and time, of bodies and intelligence.

The overturning of all existing economies, first and foremost the work-based economy, could have been anticipated.

[44] Norbert Wiener, 'Cybernetics, or Control and Communication', in *The Man and The Machine*, 1948: 'The Human Use of Human Beings', in *Cybernetics and Human Beings*, 1950.

Often, over the following years and even decades, it has been surprising to see all regimes, governments and parties ignore this in their analyses or in their medium- and long-term planning. They discussed work, industry, unemployment and the economy without ever considering those phenomena which seemed such determining factors, obviously holding potentialities which then seemed to herald (and could have heralded) unhoped-for perspectives. In 1980, again, I could write: 'It is surprising that cybernetics has not been developed under *any* regime. That the same outworn, oppressive market is always settled for. Cybernetics is not necessarily a "solution", but to ignore it as a possibility does look like a symptom. Lack of imagination? Too much imagination rather! And terrified at the idea of freedom ...'[45] For the idea of the end of work or anything taking that path could not at the time be regarded as anything but a liberation.

Neglected by politics, cybernetics was therefore introduced into the economy almost absent-mindedly, without strategic thinking or Machiavellian ulterior motives, but so to speak innocently, with practical ends and no theories, more like a simple tool useful at first and soon indispensable. It could have been anticipated but was not; it turned out to be a factor of incommensurable scope and great importance, responsible for a revolution of a planetary nature. Inscribed in our habits, its consequences should have been most beneficial to all, almost miraculous. They have been disastrous.

Far from opening up the way to a welcome and concerted decline and even abolition of work, cybernetics gave rise to its scarcity without eliminating, or even modifying, the necessity of working, or the networks of vital exchanges in which work is always supposed to be the single connecting factor.

The initial innocence of businesses and markets gave way to far more lucid and better planned utilization of the new

---

[45] *La Violence du calme.*

technologies, and then to a most energetic management aimed at the profit that could be expected from them, and for which flesh-and-blood workers are paying the price.

Far from representing a relief beneficial to all and close to a heaven-like fantasy, the fading away of work is becoming a threat, and its scarcity, its precariousness have become disasters. Very illogically and cruelly, even murderously, work is still desperately necessary – not to society or even productivity now, but to the survival itself of those who are *not* working, and who cannot get work any more, and for whom work only would mean salvation.

In such a context is it easy for those who are the most fragile (the great majority) to admit that work itself is doomed, and that but for the obsolete utility it retains for them, but for the vital necessity it means to them, it has hardly any reason to exist any more? Even if proof and examples are proferred constantly?

And then when the fact has indeed been reiterated over and over since the mists of time: the fact that we have no other utility than that conferred on us by work, or rather employment, by the purpose for which we are employed, how could it be assimilated that work itself is no longer useful, is useless, not even useful for profit or even worthy of being exploited?

The sublimation, glorification and deification of work derive from all this, not only from the material distress caused by its absence. If the Almighty were to curse mankind today, saying: 'In the sweat of thy face shalt thou eat bread', it would be heard as a reward and a blessing! It seems to be forgotten forever that work was often – and not so very long ago, either – regarded as coercive, a constraint, and quite often as hell.

But did Dante ever imagine the inferno of those who would clamour in vain for hell, for whom the worst damnation would be expulsion from hell itself?

It is Shakespeare who says through Ariel's voice: 'Hell is empty, and all the devils are here.'

A way might have been opened up leading not to a want

of labour, of jobs, but to their soothing and concerted decline, a way that could have led to that disappearance as to a
relief favourable to all, to a freer, more fulfilling passage
through life. Instead, it leads to a loss of status, pauperization, humiliation and social exclusion, and perhaps the
ejection of an increasing number of human beings.

It opens up to risks of the worst. Our surges at escape, our
enthusiasm for avoidance and our reluctance to be lucid help
us to stagnate in the present drama, which could lead to a
quite more tragic situation. Yet nothing is closed off, everything is still possible. But it is most urgent to find within
what context, not yet officially official but operative, within
what configurations, what political – that is, economic –
designs and plans, above all within what consented subterfuges our lives fall today.

To achieve this we have to free ourselves from a syn-
drome, that of the 'Purloined Letter',[46] that letter put in
such an obvious place that it went unnoticed. But while in
Poe's short story the letter was concealed thanks to the ruse
of the person who wanted to hide it, it is hidden today by the
reluctance of those who should be looking for it and by their
desperate determination not to find it, or not to admit to
themselves that they have seen it, so as to make sure that
they will avoid any risk of reading it. Yet ignoring its con-
tents is no guarantee at all against what it could reveal. Quite
the contrary.

We are not as indifferent and passive as we seem. All our
strength and efforts are indeed bent on not recognizing what
prevents us and will even more prevent us from pursuing the
one kind of existence known to us, one merged with the
labour system and according to us the only kind of life
suiting this planet. We even go to the point of accepting
being deprived of it and excluded from it, so long as we can
still at least be its spectators, even of its decay.

Our resistance goes in that direction and makes us blind
and deaf precisely to what might arouse other kinds of

---

[46] By Edgar Allan Poe, first published in 1845. [trans.]

resistance, or even simple reappraisals. We steadily confine ourselves to the role of vestal virgins.

We agree to be told about 'unemployment' as if that were really the point, for when hearing the term it still sounds like an echo of the term 'work', an echo that may be one of our very last links with it.

We agree to endless increases in unemployment while we are endlessly promised that it will be brought down; we agree to the fact that those promises serve as pretexts for all abuses, and for the staging of an unbearable, planetary scene, for it makes us feel that even unwanted, even rejected, we remain within the sphere we wouldn't for anything in the world leave: that of work, the lack of work still belonging, after all, to that sphere.

We know we have entered on a different, irreversible phase of history that we know nothing of, that nobody knows, and whose existence we pretend to ignore. But isn't it strange and highly implausible that it has assumed such a mournful appearance, and that admitting the truth amounts to bereavement, so that even thinking of it and confronting it seems unendurable? Is it really so cruel to accept that we are no longer under the power of labour as it was once understood, under conditions so hard to bear at the time? But aren't we more than ever under that power and more than ever enslaved to it in its deficiency?

Logically, shouldn't liberation from the biblical curse of compulsory labour lead to more freedom in the use of our time, help to breathe again and feel alive, experience emotions without always being ordered about, exploited, dependent, and suffering such tiredness? Hasn't such a mutation been hoped for since the dawn of time, taken as an inaccessible dream, more desirable than any other?

That passage from an old order of existence to the one now being set up and that we refuse to discover seemed to be utopia-like. But whenever it was thought about, it was imagined as run by the workers themselves, by all inhabitants and not imposed by a few, by a tiny number, behaving as the masters of now useless slaves, as owners of the planet which would be theirs alone to rule and manage for their sole benefit, in their sole interests, since numbers of human auxiliaries would no longer be necessary to them.

Never would it have been imagined that deliverance from the straitjacket of labour would seem a catastrophe and that it would rise up as the sudden manifestation of an initially clandestine phenomenon. Nor was it ever guessed that a world capable of functioning without the sweat of so many brows would be immediately grabbed (or would have been so previously) and that the major concern would be to catch and corner the now superfluous workers, the better to throw them out. And that it would not result in a greater capacity for all to use, appreciate and take on a living status, but as a reinforced coercion bringing privations, humiliations, deficiencies, and above all even worse servitude through the increasingly obvious institution of an oligarchy. But also by the proclaimed improbability of any alternative and the general acquiescence and consensus reaching cosmic dimensions.

However, the lack not so much of any struggle as of any concerted criticism or any reaction is now reaching such proportions, and seems so absolute, that the decision-makers, finding no serious obstacles in the way of their plans, seem almost dizzy in the face of the dead calm of non-existent or at least unexpressed public opinion, in the face of its tacit consent confronted with really radical phenomena and events – or advents – unleashed on such a scale and with such new power and speed.

'Social cohension' appears so unshakeable, in spite of 'social fracture', that it seems to disconcert even those who fear seeing it break up, particularly since they have detected the signals likely to set off all protests unheard till now.

Hence the prudence and patience shown in their speeches. A patience and a prudence less and less necessary. From now on the ground is fully prepared, the vocabulary popularized, the ideas approved! Everything is going like clockwork.

Thus, for instance, at the G7 meeting on employment

held in Lille in April 1996, despite a brave but ineffective attempt by the French head of state, who regained a bit of the spirit of his presidential campaign and proposed at least a statement mentioning social issues, the seven most industrialized and thus richest countries in the world did not even deem deception worth while, but tranquilly agreed – and this time without the usual deviousness, circumlocution and matters left unsaid – on the absolute necessity of a deregulation, a flexibility, in short an 'adaptation' of labour to globalization, now well ratified, even commonplace, and resolutely asserting themselves outside any social context. Of course. 'Regulation' will be carried out, but nothing more. The routine will be ratified. Adaptation is going full speed ahead in the broad light of day.

It has plenty to do. At the same meeting, the head of the International Labour Organization pointed out that 'the number of unemployed in the G7 countries rose from thirteen to twenty-four million between 1979 and 1994', that is, it almost doubled in fifteen years, 'not counting the four million who have given up looking for work and the fifteen million working part-time because they have no other option'.

Quite an acceleration? Recently, what was already creeping into some analyses, a few premonitions, is being asserted clearly, as a fiat, though it is presented as an alternative, apparently allowing us to retain a degree of autonomy and even initiative: we face a choice. We have from now on the faculty to choose whether we prefer unemployment to extreme poverty, or extreme poverty to unemployment. Some dilemma! And it's no use complaining afterwards; it will have been your own decision.

But let's not be anxious: we shall have both.

They're a pair and the choice is between two models, the European one and the Anglo-Saxon one.

For some time now Anglo-Saxon countries have managed a statistical fall in the unemployment statistics thanks, among other things, to a social welfare system hovering around zero, spectacular skill in handling labour flexibility, and workfare schemes that contradict the Declaration of Human Rights principles that forbid compulsory work, and above all the fact that, according to Robert Reich,[47] a great and often visionary economist: 'The United States continues to tolerate a great disparity in incomes – the greatest in all industrialized countries – which would no doubt be intolerable in most Western European countries.' However, this 'intolerable' poverty, based on what is modestly presented as 'a great disparity' between the unspeakable indigence of an impressive number and the unparalleled opulence of a small minority, allows Robert Reich to go on: 'on the other hand, the country has opted for greater flexibility, resulting in more employment.'

So there it is.

Plainly put, one is as poor as ever, and in addition (if one dares say so), poor without social welfare and poor while working. A triumph for the principles of the OECD and other world organizations. Not only does an increased punishment of the unemployed or an accentuated destitution provide a tamed and easily manipulated labour force at minimum cost, but they also bring down the unemployment rates. This is expressed in the institutionalization of a degree of indigence scarcely credible in so powerful a country as the United States, where fortunes swell to proportions hitherto unknown – matching the growing poverty and distress, a distress shared by workers who despite (or rather because of) their wages are living below the poverty line, and by the greatly impoverished middle classes whose jobs are more and more precarious and are often mere scraps, rags or remnants of jobs, very poorly paid. And as usual without the security of any social welfare system, even for health.

But all the same it may be possible to put to work some shirkers as the OECD and the IMF were confident they would. Alas, there still remain countless other lazy lie-abeds sleeping on the pavements sheltered by their cardboard boxes, or taking it easy standing in line outside employment

---

[47] Clinton's first Secretary of Labour (*Le Monde*, 7–8 April 1996).

offices, or even lounging around, stuffing their faces in those charitable places for whose benefit 'big' business has so often gone to the trouble of dining on caviar, as is usually done to raise funds for the starving. Nothing is begrudged the poor when it comes to charity.

However, in response to the lucid observations presented by Robert Reich the economist,[48] Robert Reich the American Secretary of Labour tries, much less successfully, to find solutions. He suggests a rise in wages, but the means at his disposal to provide it suddenly become curiously vague. He dreams of endlessly rehashed training sessions, lifelong education, and other outworn gadgets. But he also utters a word which seems to have a new ring and to be promised to a great future: 'employability', which turns out to be a very close relative of flexibility, even one of the forms it takes.

To wage-earners, it means being available for every kind of change, for the whims of fate, in this case those of the employers. They'll have to expect to change jobs over and over. But to offset the certainty of being tossed 'from job to job', they will have a *reasonable* guarantee'[49] – i.e., no guarantee – 'of finding a job different from the previous and lost one, but with the same wage'. It all brims over with fine sentiments, but trailing from one more or less casual job to jobs more or less casual is nothing new, and as for *reasonable* guarantees', one suspects they will always and immediately be regarded as *un*reasonable, and therefore null and void. However, the name of a gadget that will distract the crowds has been invented. Let's not forget it: employability.

The term will be popular. One can imagine how 'professional' the so-called 'employable' will be, the degree of interest they will bring to their work, what progress and experience they will acquire. Also their status of interchangeable pawns and professional nonentities. And this has nothing to do with a life of adventure opposed to a dreary, pen-pushing existence, but with a situation that will accen-

---

[48] *Le Monde*, 7–8 April 1996.
[49] Italics in the text of the interview.

tuate their fragility and put them even more at risk. It has to do with constantly renewed worries of undergoing constantly renewed apprenticeships without much chance of getting good. Of course, there will be no question of any actual 'profession'. With each new attempt they will have to make sure not to get disliked by people unknown to them, without much hope of having time to make friends or to find a position, a situation, a status of their own, however tiny. A true work 'place', even less. Existence will fluctuate endlessly between an obsession with not losing this particular job too soon, however undesirable and undesired it is, and having lost it, with finding another one. Despite idle hours, such obsessions will leave hardly any room for other investments, while even brightened up with a '*reasonable* guarantee', that way of life won't suggest or allow any either.

Yet some will at least be delighted at the thought that in such a landscape trade unions will no longer hold sway. Permanent comings and goings, the brevity of time spent in companies whose functioning they will have no time to grasp, being isolated elements only passing through, will render unions ineffectual. Not even possible. As for agreements, meetings, displays of solidarity, collective protests, works councils, they are just so many forgotten old things.

Permanent and general 'sub-interim' periods will be the thing for which some resounding, high-flown euphemism will most certainly be found, since an interim period is now called, at least in France, a 'mission'. James Bond all the way!

Even better! A brilliant invention: the 'zero-hour working', as practised in the United Kingdom. Employees are paid only when they work. Fair enough? Yes. But they are only employed from time to time, and meanwhile are imperatively bound to wait at home, *unpaid but at the employer's disposal*, waiting for him to summon them when he thinks good and for what he thinks the right amount of time. They must then hurry to get back to work for a limited period.

A dream-life indeed! But so what? Allowing oneself every latitude one can get anything. Also do anything. If not enough work is left for everyone, there is still a little left. But to get a chance of profiting from it you must not ask the impossible but keep to the station fallen to you, a fallen one.

In the United States, Edmund S. Phelps remarked, work is given priority over wages, while in Europe wages are over work. Perhaps. But nothing, anywhere, operates to the detriment of profit.

It all goes on within thriving markets, the essential being that they should flourish even more all the time. It will be explained to us how indispensable their prosperity is to employment and general well-being. Unless it is thought more useful not to explain anything to us.

XI

However, as an alternative to the Anglo-Saxon way, the European variant remains, with the unbridled splendours of its orgiastic social welfare system! Its welfare state famous, of course, for indulging in such expensive 'mistresses' as the homeless and unemployed kept in sinful luxury.

Large corporations and world organizations look with disapproval on these debaucheries of other times, holding them responsible for all ills: minimum wage, paid holidays, family allowances, social security, income aid and other cultural extravagances, to mention only some examples of that wastefulness. So much money filched from the sights of the free market economy to keep people who don't really expect all that. Searching for work is quite enough to fulfil any life; not finding it just adds spice. How could one not regret the squandering of all this virtual 'wealth creation' gone down the drain, when it obviously could have been used to the advantage of all, if only through the stream of jobs it was surely bound to create. How deplorable that such outworn habits can't be more swiftly eradicated.

In France, this eradication is prevented by the quiet resistance of a silent, unorganized but skittish body of opinion, vigilant, ready to react and be mobilized, and in many respects still barely committed to today's one-track thinking, sometimes even alien to it. A deep-rooted social culture including long-established, already acquired social benefits maintains an order which, although shaken and apparently losing ground, still holds to something of a human register, which persists in frequently remaining a major point of reference. Even if, globalized, as might be expected, we may be slipping more or less insensibly away from this state of law, it is still ours.

A struggle reminiscent of Monsieur Seguin's pathetic goat (in Daudet's story) fighting in vain for its life? Indeed, once again, the question, on the one hand, is how not to perish and, on the other, how to satisfy an inextinguishable appetite. Yet the question is less a matter of a struggle than a presence, a memory obstinately persisting.

The stakes are huge on both sides. The markets know how to evaluate theirs, and they have the means to defend them. Better still – for they have gone beyond that stage – they know how to avoid being restrained in their amazing advance. Within their own networks they form a united force powerful as no coalition has ever been before. The alibi of competition and competitivity they still put forward really conceals perfect mutual understanding, a dream-like cohesion, a sheer idyll.

Indeed, every company, even every country, claims to be battling the greed of its predatory rivals and pretends to be dependent on their habits and dragged into their headlong rush. It is the others, all the others, they repeat, who impose competition, foster competitiveness, and make them take the general deregulation paths they set up, involving flexible wages (that is rock-bottom wages), freedom for redundancies and the whole series of rights they all enjoy. So much so that refusing to comply with the tendency would play into their rivals' hands and mean collapse, also (and this is to be avoided at all costs; the heart sinks at the mere thought of it) dragging down jobs with them. Hence the imperative necessity of preserving jobs by sacking workers freely (that is, massively,) making wages 'flexible' (which goes without saying), relocating, and so on. In short, by doing the same as everybody and following the crowd.

The usual speech runs: 'Sorry, but what are we to do? The

rest of them are out there with their claws bared. This mad competition and a crazy world force us to go along with them if we are not to disappear, and jobs with us.' This rhetoric may be translated as: 'Thanks to our combined efforts, everything is reduced to what we think rational, equitable and profitable, all that binds us together. This world of competition is ours – initiated, controlled and managed by us. It imposes what we demand. It is inevitable and is one with us as we want, can do and take everything together.'

A new slant on the principle of, 'One for all and all for one', and to which the planetary answer is: 'Nothing for all and all for nothing.'

And always the use of blackmail as a weapon, the use of that myth of jobs which are in decline anyway, a decline stirred up with unfailing zeal by their only supposed champions.

Instead of the supposed conflicts, one and only one game is being played – by several players, it is true, but all joining forces towards the same end, within the same unspoken ideology. It takes place in the same, unique, very exclusive club where it is possible to win or lose, create clans and hierarchies, invent brand-new rules which will work to the disadvantage of some, even cheat and set traps, or help others, quarrel, even come to stabbing, but always among one's own kind, everyone agreeing on the necessity and validity of the club, on the tiny number of members admitted to it, and their dominance. And on the insignificance of those who are not part of it.

Competition? Competitiveness? They operate within the club and with all the members' consent. A private affair. They are part of the game which they actually rule, and which is none of the business of those outside the club. They are not making one population the rivals of another. On the contrary, all populations have one thing in common: they are *not* part of the club even if, with a sudden onset of familiarity, it claims them as allies, almost associates, even accomplices who would have much to lose or gain with one or

other of the so-called opponents in these pretended conflicts. In truth the game is being played without them, not to
say against them. It is a quite civilized game, organized to
ensure that every one of the assumed adversaries will always
win everything, all the time.

Competition and competitiveness do not disturb the
companies and markets as much as is said, and certainly not
as it is said. Global and transnational networks are far too
closely interlinked, intertwined and connected with each
other for that. They rather serve as alibis disguising an
interest common to the whole private economy and resid-
ing in those very advantages, privileges and requirements
and the permissivities which the private economy claims is
enjoined upon it by formidable and menacing competition,
whereas it is primarily a question of alliances within one
same programme – and a common will, splendidly managed.

Rivalries do play a large part in the market economy, but
not in the spheres or at the levels it likes to indicate. What is
claimed to be the result of competition derives, on the
contrary, from the combined will of all. Were it composed of
a single group, it would be even more focused on what works
to its advantage, the exclusion of that world of labour for
which it no longer has any use.

Hence the impatience aroused by the misplaced 'generosity' of social welfare and other disputed forms of extrava-
gance. Disputes and protests so often reiterated, so insistent,
aggressive, sure of their facts that one might end up subscrib-
ing to them before remembering how indifferent they are to
what vanishes behind the statistics: the extent of grief, the
acuteness of poverty, and the degradation of life and all hope
mutilated. They also ignore or fail to mention the fact that
the 'benefits' and 'welfare' they revile, exhibited as godsends
reserved for the privileged who shamelessly bask and wallow
in this bonanza, amount to less than is necessary for normal
survival, and keep their obliged recipients well below the
poverty line. So do many pensions, trainees' salaries, subsidized contracts, and other stratagems meant to help in

'cutting back' but in this case, cutting back the nagging unemployment statitics.

Unemployment which today is rife at all levels of all social classes, bringing distress, insecurity and a sense of shame due mainly to the aberrations of a society which regards it each time as an exception to the general rule established forever. A society which claims to be continuing along a path that no longer exists, instead of looking for others.

But meanwhile, what a curse being a unit in these statistics, grappling with the innumerable complications, mortifications and humiliations that accompany unemployment. To be in some (indeed many) cases living on the equivalent of 2,400 francs a month, or even less, or nothing when one has exhausted one's entitlement. And always the repeated and useless attempts to find a position. And the delight of receiving new confirmation every day that you are officially regarded as worthless. And with *no* position.[50]

This kind of grief is quickly said, quickly thought about but so long, so slow to live through.

Do we fully understand that the question no longer concerns only certain bullied categories of people or mere political ups and downs, but a whole system being set up, if it is not already set and evicting all or almost all of us?

An important part to play is left to the great majority, that of consumers, a role suiting everybody. Don't even the underprivileged happen, for instance, to eat noodles with famous names, names more honoured than their own? Noodles quoted on the stock exchange? Aren't we all potential players and apparently much sought after in that 'growth', which is thought to contain all the solutions?

Consumption, then, is our last resort. Our final usefulness. We are still good enough for the role of customers necessary for that 'growth' so lauded, so desired, so often promised as the end of all evils, and so feverishly awaited. What a relief! Yet playing that role and occupying that rank need the

---

[50] 2400F in 1996 = $470; £300.

means to occupy that role and status. But here is what will be a greater relief even: is there anything that won't be done to provide us with those means or to preserve those we might already have? 'The customer is king' – a sacred principle: who would dare infringe it?

But then why that methodical, organized pauperization which is said to be rational, even necessary, and even full of promises, and why does it go on increasing? Why slash almost with rage, by tens of thousands, the ranks of potential consumers supposed to be the 'geese who lay the golden eggs', those masters of 'wealth creation' who actually create so much poverty? Why is the market economy bent on sawing off the branch on which it claims to be sitting? Would it be scuttling its own ship with 'social plans', 're-structuring', wage flexibility, competitive deflation, and other frenetic projects aimed at abolishing those measures which still allow the most deprived to consume the slightest bit? Is this sheer masochism?

Let us see what growth represents in the view of that 'apostle of productivity', Stephen Roach[51] who has re-nounced his passion for 'downsizing' (but that doesn't pre-vent him from adjuring Europe to extricate itself from the Merovingian times in which it persists, and not to wax indignant): Europe 'has not even begun to envisage the kinds of strategies we have adopted in the States' ... the same strategies from which he is now backing off!

Strategies which, on the other hand, he strongly recom-mends to backward Europe, promising it alluring results. As 'the progress advances' that he describes as 'deregulation, globalization and privatization', he guarantees that 'sad as it may seem, there will inevitably be redundancies'! Whereas he is now recommending to his own country to resign itself to recruit workers, Europe, on the other hand, must abso-lutely not stop at such details: those backward countries must not on any account 'shelter behind the American expe-rience or make [his] new analysis of the situation a pretext

---

[51] *Le Monde*, 29 May 1996.

for refusing the need to restructure; [that] would mean giving up being competitive.' But of course!

This is a man of experience from a booming country! Surely it would be foolish not to turn his advice to good account and not to stop marking time, so that like him, with the same methods, we can reach the stage at which he got it all wrong! Anyway, how does he work out that he has gone astray – the way he advocates for others? First of all, he did *not* go the wrong way, well, not really: it was the others who failed to follow his prescriptions to the letter. Then again, he could not resist his own laudable inclinations: in his 'scenario of economic recovery through productivity' he envisaged, he tells us, 'an environment of weak inflation and sustained growth of profits, and thus a very positive atmosphere for shares and bonds, even if the growth of the economy was very slow'. Would growth no longer have much prestige in his eyes? Alas, doesn't Mr. Roach continue: 'Concurrently, I saw a very strong tendency to downsizing, cutting back on labour costs, which encouraged a highly constructive economic climate?' No! Growth is certainly not the main concern of this 'apostle of productivity'. Nor is purchasing power, which is so merrily 'curbed'. On the other hand, the wrecking – or failing that, the weakening – of growth and purchasing power are preconditions of an economic climate he judges 'very constructive'. One would like to hear the views of the labour force and the downsized, heroes of this success.

Thus does our 'apostle' show the prominently displayed growth factor in quite a different light, revealing the kind of enthusiasm with which it is regarded by the real economy. An enthusiasm shared by those governments eagerly slashing (in tens of thousands again), this time among the ranks of consumers that are civil servants for instance, who do not depend on the private sector but who should nevertheless be regarded as 'profitable' according to market criteria. Not regarded as necessary or competent, but as 'profitable' – by the standards of what sacred authority? And who cares if, despite the clichés so complacently reiterated presenting them as lazy 'haves', indolent profiteers and thirsty vampires, they are necessary as teachers, health workers and public employees – or even as ... consumers. The staff shortages in hospitals, schools, colleges, railways and so on is recognized, yet on grounds of cutting costs (in view of what, to obtain what else?) these very staffs are subjected to massive slimming. Here the automation that enables costs to be cut in the labour force while profits are maintained is not responsible for these redundancies, this reduction of the workforce. Contempt alone is responsible.

And also the fact (quite a remarkable one) of having managed to have that contempt shared by the very public suffering from it and subjected to its consequences.

There is a blatant contradiction between the creation of extensive precariousness and the much touted expression of a growth which is said to be ardently hoped for and presented as a remedy for all ills. Is it sure that the end in view is really *this* very kind of growth which would stem *these* ills? And not the growth of financial speculations and more or less virtual markets – 'electronic capitalism' – so dissociated from the growth in question?

In this context, however, what about advertising that seems so crucial, and which, seems so crucial, and which, seeming to top everything and making us live in a world no longer reified but labelled, where people often see their names replaced by acronyms while inanimate objects have proper names forming a population of labels haunting and obsessing the mind, focusing all impulses? So much so that, all things considered, there might be no need any more for real products corresponding to brand names.

By dint of more seductions and ruses than any courtesan, any proselyte has ever used, by means of libidinal suggestions or association, it is for labels that we are made to be overcome with desire. Our fantasies, or most subliminal reactions are dissected in public. Whether we are right- or left-wing, advertisers know how to sell us all the very same ravioli in the very same way. Or perfume, or cheese. Or unemployment. Whether we buy or not, they know we will. And what we will buy.

Perhaps the real interest of advertising increasingly lies in those functions: in the powerful distraction it causes, in the cultural environment it saturates – keeping it at the lowest level – but mainly in the deviation of desire, in this science of desire that makes it able to be packaged, that persuades us that it exists and exists only where indicated. And certainly nowhere else.

Perhaps advertising's role is becoming more political than economic, more catechistic than promotional. Perhaps it serves chiefly to suppress Mallarmé and his machine gun for good. Perhaps, unknown even to those who practise it, the role of a consumer, once drowsy, has very little importance and is not the real stake. Perhaps we are being left with that illusion as if out of politeness. Out of prudence, too and not without a certain patience: these children can be so difficult, how are you to guess what they might get up to next?

Stephen Roach too is well aware of this. If he rejoices in the fact that 'in a world where competition is increasingly intense, the employer is still the one with the power', he nevertheless sighs: 'But in the arena of public opinion the rules of the game are different: leaders of industry and share-holders are the object of unprecedented attacks.' One all the same wonders whether he might not be fantasizing a little about the importance and potential consequences of these attacks. But what is mainly interesting to note is that any resistance does make a mark, since Mr Roach finds himself obliged to conclude: 'The fact is, you cannot keep squeezing the labour force like a lemon.' Here, you can almost hear the tears in his voice.

Meanwhile, clearance is the thing. Staffing levels are enthusiastically cut on all sides, while, out of politeness again, a brighter and working future is proclaimed and promised. Living standards are undermined while trust is recommended. Institutions are broken up, social benefits eroded, but each time to preserve them and give them a last chance. 'It's for your own good, my child!'

All this in the name of catastrophes lying in wait, as so many swords of Damocles. We are told about them without much detail, by mentions of 'deficits' and 'shortfalls' which must urgently be made up. Panic is managed, but according to what? What exactly are these calamities, supposedly ready to overwhelm and devour us . . . as long as we do not let ourselves be devoured first by those who proclaim them? What precise information are we given? What monster, for instance, does that 'deficit' represent? What disaster, exactly, would be worse than those fomented by the measures designed to remedy it? Can no possible alternative at least be envisaged, even if the same course has to be taken in the end? What is the aim in view? The smooth running of the markets, or the well-being, even the survival, of populations?

Anyway, that missing money exists. Even if divided up very particularly, it exists! But let's not dwell on this point; it would hardly be 'proper'. This is nothing but a simply remark in passing, and passing very quickly. . . .

Musn't the basic principle be respected at all costs: public opinion must not be upset? Its silence must not be disturbed. That silence that makes one wonder how it was obtained. 'Strength reigns over the world, not public opinion. But it is public opinion that uses strength.' Pascal's voice can be recognized. But obviously Pascal is not and never was part of big business.

What, then, is the aim of this vague but methodical disorder, this economic anarchy, this 'dogma of *laissez -faire*'[52] irresistibly sweeping us out of the scope of our lives, out of life?

Isn't it obvious that nothing is happening or decided on the stage we are made to watch, the one we are on, while everything around is bustling so as to have us believe the opposite?

Is it still possible to make other choices than those not related to the epiphenomena of decisions already taken within a single system, already globally established while we barely start (but so faintly) to be aware of it? Would it be

---

[52] Karl Polanyi, *Origins of Our Time: The Great Transformation* (London 1944).

conceivable to suggest – only suggest – any course that might seem to run, however slightly, against the interests of the private markets (or even that might not seem to rush exactly in their direction) without hearing immediate objections? That is if time has been left for such suggestions to be made: 'Good heavens! If they so much as hear such an idea they'll be off. They'll decamp, vacate the scene, clear out, skedaddle, do a bolt, make for the hills bag and baggage!' 'They', as may be gathered, refers to our beloved big business leaders, so fickle, so fleet of foot, volatile, and ever ready to take flight along with their companies and their few remaining jobs, those threatened, or rather threatening scraps (in fact with all the threats and blackmail linked to employment). To take flight towards these 'elsewheres' in which wise, subjected populations, 'adapted' nations are permanently awaiting them.

There is no country unaware of the aptitude of the ruling circles to leave any nation (particularly their own) and go to more docile ones. There is no country that doesn't wish to be on their list of respectable places, and that has not converted itself into a municipality in the global world.

The same game, therefore, is played everywhere. Not a corner of the world has gone uninvested. Everywhere – and more and more in this dissolute Europe now energetically brought to its senses – speeches announce the reduction of public expenditure (failing its abolition), the organization of massive redundancies, increased flexibility of labour. But everywhere also the same leitmotifs punctuate these speeches, maintaining that the chief purpose of this globalized scheme, which is setting up and fostering an authoritarian economic system indifferent to the inhabitants of this world – and by nature antagonistic to their useless presence, which is already close to being parasitical, since it is now 'unprofitable', maintaining that the chief purpose of these manifestly harmful measures is – it goes without saying – to 'fight unemployment' and 'fight for employment'.

Leitmotifs formulated more and more mechanically, with increasing nonchalance, as no one is fooled. On the contrary, everyone seems curiously complicit: both those who kindly go on taking the trouble to use courteous periphrasis in addressing populations who no longer can give their opinion but who demand those promises, endure their perjuries, and after all ask nothing but to be exploited – and those populations who, like children, are always asking for the same story. A story they do not believe but pretend to do so, afraid as they are of silence and of what goes unsaid, which they guess but do not want to know.

A refusal ever to hear or see that everything is conspiring to plan their absence, that everything is shrinking and getting desertic, that the signals coming from a world reduced to being merely economic really seem to warn us that we represent the superfluous expense of that economy.

That very expense that one lies in wait for so as to chase it away, wishing forever to eliminate it. And what if it involves human beings? Current morality demands first that the balance sheets be irreproachable. It is a matter of ethics.

XII

Thus, under tacit threat, we are being immobilized in condemned social areas, in these anachronistic places that selfdestruct, but where we are so desperately, so curiously longing to stay, while the future is organized before our very eyes on the basis of our assumed and already more or less knowingly planned absence.

We are ready to do anything on earth to ignore it. Anything rather than grasping the more and more systematic ostracization, this relegation within a disintegrating system, while a contemporary age is being set up that does not synchronize with us. Anything rather than registering the gap between a market economy which is now sole proprietor of this world and those who inhabit it, prisoners of its geography. Anything rather than taking this break in continuity to be real, particularly when the leaders and strategists of the new (if unproclaimed) regime address us, through the intermediary of the political class, in terms that still respond to our codes, while their verbosity lulls and reassures us.

Now, if the masters of this economy persist in ruining what is already ruined, exploiting the vestiges of a vanished era, managing life according to their own microcosm, at the time of new era to which their contemporaries have no access, and above all if they persist in regarding the work they are eliminating (not without making sure it appears to keep its values) as the key of life, they may well end up finding the answer to their as yet inchoate question about their fellow creatures. 'How to get rid of them?' But that is a story they themselves probably unconsciously ignore just as they are unaware of the dangers they threaten us with, and meeting with no resistance, to boot. And that passivity seems to be the most unexpected fact. Such lack of interest, such resignation and globalized apathy are what might let in the worst. The worst which stands at our gates.

There have certainly been periods of more bitter distress and of even more harsh destitution, more unbridled atrocities and infinitely more conspicuous cruelty; there never was any so coldly, widely and radically dangerous.

While social ferocity has always existed, it had imperative limits, because labour resulting from human lives was indispensable to those who held power. It is not any more. Instead, it has become a burden and those boundaries are collapsing. Do we fully understand what that means? Never has humanity as a whole been so threatened in its very survival.

Whatever the history of barbarism over the centuries, human beings until now were always given a guarantee: they were essential to the function of the planet as well as to productivity, and to the exploitation of the instruments of profit – of which they themselves were part. So many elements that protected them.

For the first time, the mass of humanity is no longer materially and even less economically necessary to the small number holding power, and for whom human lives outside their private circle have nothing to recommend them, even have no existence – it is more obvious every day – but as utilitarian assets.

The balance of power, until now always latent, is shattered. Gone are the safeguards. Human lives are no more directed to public benefit. Yet it is precisely by their utility to a now autonomous economy that they are assessed. The danger lurks, as yet a virtual one, but *absolute*.

In the course of history, the human condition has often been more ill-treated than today, but by societies in need of the living in order to exist: of subaltern living people in huge numbers.

Such is no longer the case. That's why it is so serious – in a democracy and in a time when both the experience of horror and better means than ever before for social lucidity have been acquired – yes, so serious to observe the inexorable rejection of those who are no longer necessary, not to other human beings but to a market economy for which they aren't a potential source of profit any more. And it is clear they never will be again.

The opprobrium in which they are maintained, the punishment they have to suffer as if it were taken for granted, the arrogant and casual violence they are subjected to, the consent or the indifference, the passivity of all, themselves included, in the face of increasing misfortune, could be the forerunners of unlimited drifts, for the molested masses are no longer necessary to the purposes of their tormentors.

The danger is clear which, at the very least, threatens them in the short or the long term while, unconscious (or trying their best to be), they mean to remain and are mentally within a dynamic contradicted by the facts. And where employment would still be the norm and unemployment an ephemeral consequence of capricious events. The fact that unemployment is nowadays the unofficial established norm seems to escape job-seekers as well as society, official speeches or legislation. While allusions to it are (barely) beginning to be made, they will usually only be followed by paradoxical promises of a bustling future where wages and full employment will sing together, or by convoluted and verbose plans for restoring to its original state the system that has led to its self-destruction.

So why desperately and at all costs try to stick work where it is no longer needed? Why not abandon the very notion of what betrays us, is retreating or has already escaped work as we understand it? Why is employment seen as a must? That employment of men devoted to their own 'employment' at any price, even that of their ruin (since there is no more employment, since at best it is fading away)? Why act as if there could exist no other possible use of their lives of life, than to be used in this way?

Why isn't it even envisaged to try to adapt to the demands of globalization by trying not to be subjected to it but to get disengaged from it? Why not look first for a mode of *distribution and survival that would not depend on wages*? Why not look for and demand a meaning to the 'employment' of life – that of humanity as a whole – other than the employment of the whole of individuals by a few others, all the more as even that is turning out to be impossible from now on?

Indeed, there are many reasons why not. Let us cite a few of the major ones.

First, the difficulty and scope of such an undertaking which would be in the nature of a metamorphosis. Then, the interest of the economic powers in concealing precisely the camouflage they have brought about or emphasized, giving the illusion that work's presence is only temporarily interrupted – an interval certainly regarded as detestable, but that they swear they will cut short. A deception, a mirage created for the purpose of ascendancy over the great, indeed the immense number who are maintained in a precarious condition, in an impasse which renders them liable to ruthless exploitation. Then again, a desire to exploit what vestiges of human labour still remain, while preserving social cohesion built upon failure and shame, upon the cold and repressed terror of crowds sequestrated in the outdated and now destructive logic of work, or work that is no more.

Another reason: the sincere and general puzzlement, no doubt shared even by the leaders of a carnivorous economy, in the face of a new and disconcerting form of civilization, particularly when the old form has to be relinquished in such a sudden and drastic way. It is a lot to ask, and to ask of everyone, faced with that metamorphosis, that passage into another era, to succeed in adapting to it: to possess or find the necessary resources so as also to transform human nature, its most pregnant culture, and its way of thought, of meaning, acts and distribution. And thus to preserve without damage the life of the living.

The living, incredulous but as if acquiescent, seem to be spectators of their own evacuation from globalized planning, hastening to see their tragic, precarious social plight as the logical, even banal result of lacunae and mistakes for which they alone would be responsible and for which they alone must pay. Even to see it as fate.

Resignation may be due to the repression of a crushing discovery, impossible to apprehend: that of the only real, if dramatically reductive and strongly deceptive, value placed on them now, and no doubt in the past as well, a value measured by their economic 'returns' as distinct from any other quality, so that they are evaluated *below* the level of machinery. And which leaves them with no other rights, not even, in fact, the right to live – other than those connected with their work, while the circumstances that gave them access to those rights are breaking down.

Their giving up is also due to a sense of no longer having any means of pressure faced with a coercive cohesion holding power and seeming to them, wrongly, to have cropped up, sudden and indecipherable, unexpected.

A sense of stupor rather reminiscent of the despondent state of populations colonized by men who had, for better or worse, reached a historical phase different from that of those still vibrant societies they invaded and whose civilizations were invalidated by theirs. The scorned values of indigenous populations became ineffective in the very places they had developed, where only yesterday they had blossomed but where they now found themselves defeated, as if in exile, facing a power establishing itself, without giving them the means to enter freely, as equals, into the new system forcibly imported and without giving them the right to any rights.

The usurpers, on the other hand, granted themselves all rights over those who, hanging outside their ways of life, of thought, of belief and knowledge, henceforth without landmarks, literally stupefied, ended up by losing their energy and all possibilities, but even more all desire, including that of understanding, and *a fortiori* resisting. Wise and knowledgeable peoples whose wisdom, science and values are recognized today, who were often good warriors, and who faded out, locked into a predatory civilization which was not theirs and rejected them. Petrified and paralysed, ossified populations in limbo between two eras, living in a previous age, in other chronologies than those of their conquerors, who inflicted their own present on them without in any way sharing it. All this happening in places which, being their whole world, representing all they knew and imagined of the world became their prison since, for them, nowhere else existed.

Doesn't that ring a bell?

Aren't we in a rather similar way bewildered, trapped in a familiar world but in the grip of one unfamiliar to us: under the global influence of a one-track way of thinking, which no longer keeps the same time as ours and doesn't respond to our chronologies but whose timetable is dominant? A world with no elsewhere since it is entirely under that hold, but a world to which we desperately cling and fiercely persevere in remaining its pained subjects, forever dazzled by its beauty, by its offerings, its exchanges and henceforth haunted by the memory of the time when, immersed in work, we could still declare: 'We shan't die, we are too busy.'

Today we are only at the stage of surprise, of a certain wasting away, of preparation. The tragedy is not yet spectacular. Nonetheless, at the very heart, at the very core of what is held to be the acme of civilization, some 'civilized' people exclude those who are no longer suitable, and whose numbers we know are to increase in proportions hard to imagine. 'Others' are still tolerated, but fewer and fewer of them, and with increasing impatience, in increasingly harsh conditions, according to points of view more and more explicitly brutal. Alibis and excuses are not sought so much any more: the system is taken for granted. Founded on the dogma of profit, it is beyond the laws, which it deregulates if need be.

Nowadays, already the areas where the human condition is still unenthusiastically taken into account – in such cautious ways, with such reluctance, as if regretfully and with remorse – those areas are pointed out and reviled by the Gary Beckers, and implicitly disapproved of by such organizations as the World Bank and other OECDs, not to mention the fans of that one-track thinking who, united with big business apply themselves to making such eccentrics see reason. Successfully, too.

Facing this, what forces of opposition are there? None. The ways open up, without drama, to simpering barbarities, to looting perpetrated in white gloves.

This is only a start. One must pay very careful attention to such beginnings: they never seem criminal at first, nor even really dangerous. They unfold with the assent of most charming people, with good manners and fine feelings, people who would never hurt a fly, and who, what's more, if they ever find the time to think about it, regard certain situations as most regrettable but alas inevitable, and who do not understand that it is *here* at this very point that history is getting recorded. History they will not have noticed when it was hatched, when the premises of events that would later by called 'unspeakable' were occurring.

No doubt it is through events of that nature, unperceived in their own time or rather censored and blanked out of the conscious mind that history often takes shape. Events that will become later – too late – the legible signs that were hardly noticed at the time.

Maybe not having understood from the start what the fate of our sacrificed contemporaries, regarded as a nameless flock, meant, yes, maybe once they have suffered all the resulting trials that will have spread, always more permissive, maybe – if they ever come to an end – we shall find ourselves saying once again that such trials were 'unspeakable' and that 'we must never forget.' But we will not be able to forget: we will never have known.

And perhaps there will remain someone in a situation to say, 'never again.' But perhaps, one day, there will be no one left even able to think it.

Are these exaggerations? That is what is thought 'before', when it would still be time to know that only one insult, the injury of only one nail or only one hair, can set off the worst. And that the crimes *against* humanity are always crimes *of* humanity. Perpetrated *by* humanity.

The twentieth century has taught us that nothing lasts, not even the most cast-iron regimes. But also that anything is possible in the realm of ferocity. A ferocity which is henceforth more apt than ever to rage, unbridled. It is obvious that today the new technologies would provide it with multiplied means next to which previous atrocities would seem to have been nothing but timid rough drafts.

How can we avoid the thought of possible scenarios under a totalitarian regime which would have little difficulty in 'globalizing' itself and would have at its disposal the means of elimination of such efficiency, range and rapidity as never before imagined: genocides ready to go.

But perhaps it will be thought a pity not to take more advantage of the flocks of human beings and not to keep them alive for various purposes. For instance, as reserves of organs for transplants: human livestock on the hoof, stocks of live organs to be drawn upon at will for the needs of the privileged by the system.

Is that an exaggeration? But who among us screams on learning that in India, for instance, the poor sell their organs (kidneys, corneas, etc.) so as to subsist for a while? It is known. There are buyers. It is known too. It is happening today. The trade exists, and from the richest, most 'civilized' parts of the world customers can make their purchases at bargain prices. It is known that in some countries such organs are stolen – through kidnapping or murder – and there are clients for them. It is known. Who screams, other than the victims? What outcries are raised against sex tourism? Only the consumers react: they rush to the scene. It is known. And it is known that rather than the epiphenomena represented by sex tourism or the sale of human organs, the phenomena at their source should be attacked: the poverty which, let us repeat it, spurs the have-nots to undergo mutilation for the benefit of the haves, only to survive a little longer. And this is accepted. Tacitly accepted. And we live in a democracy. We are free, we are numerous. Yet who moves a finger except to fold up a newspaper or switch the television off, obeying the injunction to remain confident, smiling, entertaining and enraptured (when not already hidden, defeated and ashamed) although meanwhile, gravity and seriousness are at work, invisible, secret and harmful. At work in an almost universal silence interrupted by the chatter promising to cure what is already dead.

Speeches upon speeches announce 'employment' which does not and will not materialize. Speakers and audiences, candidates and voters, politicians and the public at large are all aware of it but they join their forces around such incantations in order, for their various reasons, to ignore or deny this knowledge.

This attitude, which flees despair by means of lies, camouflage, aberrant evasions, is both desperate and despairing. Instead, taking the risk of precision, of stating the facts, even if they lead to a certain despair is the only gesture which, lucid about the present, may preserve the future. It allows for the time being, the strength to speak, think and tell. To try and be lucid, to live at least with dignity. With 'intelligence'. And not in shame and fear, holed up in a trap from which nothing is permitted to escape any more.

To be afraid of fear, afraid of despair means opening up the paths of blackmail we know only too well.

Speeches overlooking or falsifying the real problems, diverting them to other, artificial issues, speeches constantly churning out the same promises that cannot be kept, *those* very speeches are backward-going, and endlessly stirring up the nostalgia they exploit. Those very speeches are desperate as they no longer even dare to approach or risk despair, which is our only chance of seeing the capacity to fight reborn. They also prevent the difficult task of mourning such landmarks as were, among others, wages that appraised you, dates that punctuated the emptiness of time with schedules, holidays, retirement – solid, coercive calendars which often offered within the warmth of groups the illusion of saturating time, and thereby of standing in the way of death.

It is *those* very speeches that play into the hands of populist authoritarian parties, which always know how to tell more and better lies. Daring to think with precision, daring to say what everyone dreads – while suffering from pretending to ignore it and from seeing it ignored – that alone might still bring some trust.

It is not a question of moaning over what has gone, nor is it a question of denying or refusing globalization and the boom of technologies:[53] those are facts, and they could have been elating, and not solely for business circles. The point is, *on the contrary*, to take them into account. The point is not to be colonized any more. To live in full knowledge of the facts and not to accept economic and political analyses that skim over these facts, mentioning them only as so many threatening elements forcing the adoption of cruel measures, which will only get worse if they are not accepted meekly.

Such analyses, or rather peremptory summaries, make it seem that modernity is reserved for the leading spheres of society, can be applied only to the free market economy and are effective only when in the hands of its decision-makers. Elsewhere, people are supposed to go on living in the old way, in a kind of *Son et Lumière*, in a retrospective show where the present plays no role and can confer none, where they are relegated within a system no longer running, and where they are condemned.

Facing that, it is strange all the same that no thought has ever been given to organizing society starting precisely from the absence of work instead of causing so much sterile and perilous suffering by denying its disappearance and pretending that we are only going through a mere interlude which can be ignored, or which it is claimed can be filled or even eliminated within most imprecise deadlines and time limits, endlessly extended, while despair and danger are settling in.

---

[53] Nor, in another context, to eliminate or even to disown the makeshift efforts made to decrease, however slightly, what is called 'unemployment'. The merest positive result influencing the present to anyone's advantage, is only too precious, but only so long as it is presented for what it is, not used to shore up deception and prolong anaesthesia.

Promises of a resurrection of ghosts, which will help to exert always more pressure while there is still time, or to push aside those, always more numerous, that the absence of employment might soon reduce to slavery if it hasn't already done so. Or even might force into disappearance. Into elimination.

Rather than waiting in disastrous circumstances for the fulfilment of promises that will not materialize, rather than watching out vainly and in distress for the return of work and galloping employment, would it be extravagant to try to make life decent and viable by other means and to do it *today* for those who, in what might soon be the radical absence of work or rather employment, are regarded as fallen, excluded and superfluous?

There is hardly any time left to include those lives, our lives, in their own, their true meaning: quite simply that of life, its dignity, its rights. Hardly any time is left to free them from the sweet will of those who scorn them.

Would it be extravagant to hope, at long last, not for some love – so vague, so easy to declare, so self-satisfied, authorizing itself to use all kind of punishment – but instead, for the boldness of a harsh, unrewarding sentiment, a sentiment of intractable rigour which refuses all exceptions: respect?

Bibliography

Adret, *Travailler deux heures par jour*. Paris: Seuil, 1979.

Albert, Michel, *Capitalisme contre capitalisme*. Paris: Seuil, 1991. In English: *Capitalism against capitalism*, trans. Paul Havilland. London: Whurr, 1993.

Alvi Geminello, *Le Siècle américain en Europe (1916–1933)*. Paris: Grasset, 1995.

André, Catherine and Sicot, Dominque, *Le Chômage dans les pays industrialisés*. Paris: Syros, 1994.

Arendt, Hannah, *The Human Condition*. Chicago: University of Chicago Press, 1958.

Arendt, Hannah, *Imperialism*. New York: Harcourt Brace, 1968.

Attali, Jacques, *Les Trois Mondes*. Paris: Fayard, 1981.

Attali, Jacques, *Lignes d'horizon*. Paris: Fayard, 1990.

Balandier, Georges, *Pour en finir avec le XXe siècle*. Paris: Fayard, 1994.

Bandt, Jacques de, Dejours, Christophe and Dubar, Claude, *La France malade du travail*. Paris: Bayard, 1995.

Baudrillard, Jean, *Les Stratégies fatales*. Paris: Grasset, 1983. In English: *Fatal Strategies*, trans. Philip Beitchman and W. G. J. Niesluchowski. New York: Semiotext, and London: Pluto, c.1990.

Baudrillard, Jean, *Le Crime parfait*. Paris: Galilée, 1995.

Bernard, Philippe, *L'Immigration*. Paris: Le Monde-Marabout, 1994.

Bernoux, Philippe, *La Sociologie des entreprises*. Paris: Seuil, 1995.

Bidet, Jacques and Texier, Jacques (eds), *La Crise du travail*. Paris: PUF, 1995.

Bihr, Alain and Pfefferkorn, Roland, *Déchiffrer les inégalités*. Paris: Syros, 1995.

Boissonat, Jean (report on commission headed by), *Le Travail dans 20 ans*. Paris: Odile Jacob, 1995.

Bourdieu, Pierre, *La Misère du monde*. Paris: Seuil, 1993. In English: *The Weight of the World*. Cambridge: Polity Press, forthcoming.

Bourguignat, Henri, *La Tyrannie des marchés, essai sur l'économie virtuelle*. Paris: Economica, 1995.

Brie, Christian de, 'Au carnaval des prédateurs'. *Le Monde diplomatique* (March 1995).

Brisset, Claire (ed.), preface by Martine Aubry, *Pauvretés*. Paris: Hachette, 1996.

Burguière, André and Revel, Jacques (eds), *Histoire de la France*. Paris: Seuil, 1989.

Camus, Renaud, *Qu'il n'y a pas de problème de l'emploi*. Paris: POL, 1994.

Cassen, Bernard, 'Chômage, des illusions au bricolage'. *Le Monde diplomatique* (October 1995).

Castel, Robert, *Les Métamorphoses de la question sociale: une chronique du salariat*. Paris: Fayard, 1995.

Castro, Josué de, *Géographie de faim*. Paris: Seuil, 1961. In English: *Geography of hunger*. London, Gollancz, 1952.

Chanchabi, Brahim, Chanchabi, Hedi and Spire, Juliette Wasserman, *Rassemblance, Un siècle d'immigration en Île-de-France*. Aidda, CDRII, Ecomusée de Fresnes, 1993.

Charlot, Bernard, Bartier, Elisabeth and Roche, Jean-Yves, *École et savoirs dans les banlieues de Paris*. Paris: Armand Colin, 1992.

Chatagner, François, *La Protection sociale*. Paris: Le Monde-Marabout, 1993.

Chauvin, Michel, *Tiers monde, la fin des idées reçues*. Paris: Syros, 1991.

Chesnais, François, *La Mondialisation du capital*. Paris: Syros, 1994.

Chossudovsky, Michel, 'Sous la coupe de la dette'. *Le Monde diplomatique* (July 1995).

Clerc, Denis, Lipietz, Alain and Satre-Buisson, Joël, *La Crise*. Paris: Syros, 1985.

Closets, François de (ed.), *Le Pari de la responsabilité*. Paris: Payot, 1989.

Closets, François de, *Le Bonheur d'apprendre et comment on l'assassine*. Paris: Seuil, 1996.

Colombani, Jean-Marie, *La Gauche survivra-t-elle au social-isme?* Paris, Flammarion, 1994.

Cotta, Alain, *L'Homme au travail*. Paris: Fayard, 1987.

Cotta, Alain, *Le Capitalisme dans tous ses états*. Paris: Fayard, 1991.

Courtieu, Guy, *L'Entreprise, société féodale*. Paris: Seuil, 1975.

Daniel, Jean, *Voyage au bout de la nation*. Paris: Seuil, 1995.

Debray, Régis, *Le Pouvoir intellectuel en France*. Paris: Ramsay, 1979.

Debray, Régis, *L'État séducteur: les révolutions médiologiques du pouvoir*. Paris: Gallimard, 1993.

Decornoy, Jacques, 'Travail, capital . . . pour qui chantent les lendemains'. *Le Monde diplomatique* (September 1995).

Defalvard, Hervé (ed.), *Essai sur le marché*. Paris: Syros, 1995.

Derrida, Jacques, *Spectres de Marx: l'état de la dette, le travail du deuil et la nouvelle Internationale*. Paris: Galilée, 1993.

Desanti, Jean-Toussaint, *Le Philosophe et les pouvoirs*. Paris: Calmann-Lévy, 1976.

Dubet, François and Lapeyronnie, Didier, *Les Quartiers d'exil*. Paris: Seuil, 1992.

Duby, Georges, *An 100, An 2000, sur les traces de nos peurs*. Paris: Textuel, 1995.

Duhamel, Alain, *Les Peurs françaises*. Paris: Flammarion, 1993.

Dumont, Louis, *Homo aequalis: genèse et épanouissement de l'idéologie économique*. Paris: Gallimard, 1985.

Esprit, 'L'Avenir du travail' (August–September 1995).

Ewald, François, *L'Etat-providence*. Paris: Grasset, 1986.

Ezine, Jean-Louis, *Du train où vont les jours*. Paris: Seuil, 1994.

Faye, Jean-Pierre, *Langages totalitaires: la raison critique de l'économie narrative*. Paris: Hermann, 1980.

Field, Michel, *Jours de manifs*. Paris: Textuel, 1996.
Finkielkraut, Alain, *La Défaite de la pensée*. Paris: Gallimard, 1989.
Fitoussi, Jean-Paul, *Le Débat interdit: monnaie, Europe, pauvreté*. Paris: Arléa, 1995.
Fitoussi, Jean-Paul and Rosenvallon, Pierre, *Le Nouvel Age des inégalités*. Paris: Seuil, 1996.
Flaubert, Gustave, *Madame Bovary*. Paris: Gallimard (Pléiade edn, vol. 1).
Forrester, Viviane, *La Violence du calme*. Paris: Seuil, 1980.
Forrester, Viviane, *Van Gogh ou l'enterrement dans les blés*. Paris: Seuil, 1983.
Forrester, Viviane, *Ce soir, après la guerre*. Paris: Lattès, 1992; new edn, Paris: Fayard, 1997.
Fretillet, Jean-Paul and Veglio, Catherine, *Le GATT démystifié*. Paris: Syros, 1994.
Friedmann, Georges, *Où va le travail humain?* Paris: Gallimard, 1967.
Furet, François, *Le Passé d'une illusion*. Paris: Robert Laffont/Calmann-Lévy, 1995.
Galéano, Eduardo, 'Vers une société de l'incommunication'. *Le Monde diplomatique* (January 1996).
Gauchet, Marcel, *Le Désenchantement du monde, une histoire politique de la religion*. Paris: Gallimard, 1985.
Gauchet, Marcel, *La Révolution des droits de l'homme*. Paris: Gallimard, 1989.
George, Suzan and Sabelli, Fabrizio, *Crédits sans frontières*. Paris: La Découverte, 1994.
Gorz, André, *Métamorphoses du travail: quête du sens*. Paris: Galilée, 1988.
Groupe de Lisbonne, *Limites à la compétitivité*. Paris: La Découverte, 1995.
Guetta, Bernard, *Géopolitique*, Paris: Éditions de l'Olivier, 1995.
Guillebaud, Jean-Claude, *La Trahison des lumières*. Paris: Seuil, 1995.
Halimi, Serge, 'Les Chantiers de la démolition sociale'. *Le Monde diplomatique* (July 1994).
Hassoun, Martine and Rey, Frédéric, *Les Coulisses de l'emploi*. Paris: Arléa, 1995.
Henry, Michel, *La Barbarie*. Paris: Grasset, 1987.
Iribarne, Philippe d', *La Logique de l'honneur. Gestion des entreprises et traditions nationales*. Paris: Seuil, 1989.
Iribarne, Philippe d', *Le Chômage paradoxal*. Paris: Seuil, 1990.
Jalée, Pierre, *Le Pillage du tiers monde*. Paris: Maspero, 1961.
Jeanneney, Jean-Marcel, *Vouloir l'emploi*. Paris: Odile Jacob, 1994.
Jeanneney, Jean-Noël, *Écoute la France qui gronde*. Paris: Arléa, 1996.
Jues, Jean-Paul, *La Rémunération globale des salaires*. Paris: PUF (Que sais-je?, no. 2932), 1995.
Julien, Claude, 'Capitalisme, libre échange et pseudo-diplomatie: un monde à vau-l'eau?' *Le Monde diplomatique* (September 1995).
Julliard, Jacques, *Autonomie ouvrière. Études sur le syndicalisme d'action directe*. Paris: Seuil, 1988.
Julliard, Jacques, *Ce fascisme qui vient . . .* Paris: Seuil, 1994.
Kahn, Jean-François, *La Pensée unique*. Paris: Fayard, 1995.
Keynes, John Maynard, *The General Theory of Employment, Interest and Money*. 1936, second edn. London: Routledge, 1997.
Labbens, Jean, *Sociologie de la pauvreté*. Paris: Gallimard, 1978.
Lafargue, Paul, *Le Droit à la paresse: réfutation du droit au travail de 1848*. Paris: Maspero, 1987.

Le Débat, 'L'État-providence dans la tourmente. Repenser la lutte contre le chômage?' 89 (March–April 1996).

Le Goff, Jean-Pierre, *Le Mythe de l'entreprise*. Paris: La Découverte, 1992.

Le Goff, Jean-Pierre, and Caillé, Alain, *Le Tournant de décembre*. Paris: La Découverte, 1996.

Lesourne, Jacques, *Vérités et mensonges sur le chômage*. Paris: Odile Jacob, 1995.

Lévy, Bernard-Henri, *L'Idéologie française*. Paris: Grasset, 1981.

Lévy, Bernard-Henri, *La Pureté dangereuse*. Paris: Grasset, 1994.

Magazine littéraire, 'Les exclus'. No. 334.

Mamou-Mani, Alain, *Au-delà du profit*. Paris: Albin Michel, 1995.

Manent, Pierre, *Histoire intellectuelle du libéralisme*. Paris: Calmann-Lévy, 1987. In English: *An Intellectual History of Liberalism*, trans. Rebecca Balinksi. Princeton: Princeton University Press, c.1994.

Manière de voir, 'Les nouveaux maîtres du monde'. *Le Monde diplomatique*, 28 (1995).

Mazel, Olivier, *Les Chômages*. Paris: Le Monde-Marabout, 1993.

Méda, Dominique, *Le Travail en voie de disparition*. Paris: Aubier, 1995.

Ménanteau, Jean, *Les Banlieues*. Paris: Le Monde-Marabout, 1994.

Mignot-Lefebvre, Yvonne and Lefebvre, Michel, *Les Patrimoines du futur*. Paris: L'Harmattan, 1995.

Morin, Edgar, *L'Esprit du temps*. Paris: LGF, Livre de poche biblio, 1983.

Nora, Pierre (ed.), *Les Lieux de mémoire*. Paris: Gallimard, 1984. In English: *Realms of Memory*, trans. Arthur Goldhammer. New York: Columbia University Press, 1996.

Norel, Philippe, *Les Banques face aux pays endettés*. Paris: Syros, 1990.

Norel, Philippe and Saint-Alary, Éric, *L'Endettement du tiers monde*. Paris: Syros, 1988.

OECD, *Jobs Study*, 1994, 1995.

Pascal, Blaise, *Pensées*. Paris: Gallimard (Pléiade edn). In English: *Pensées and Other Writings*, trans. Honor Levi. Oxford and New York, Oxford University Press.

Paugam, Serge (ed.), *L'Exclusion: l'état des savoirs*. Paris: La Découverte, 1996.

Perret, Bernard, *L'Avenir du travail*. Paris: Seuil, 1995.

Perrin-Martin, J.-P. (ed.), preface by Alfred Grosser, *La Rétention*. Paris: L'Harmattan, 1996.

Petrella, Riccardo, 'Le retour des conquérants'. *Le Monde diplomatique* (March 1995).

Phelps, Edmund S., *Political Economy*. New York: Norton, c.1985.

Piot, Olivier, *Finance et économie, la fracture*. Paris: Le Monde-Marabout, 1995.

Plenel, Edwy, *La République menacée, dix ans d'effet Le Pen, 1982–1992*. Paris: Le Monde éditions, 1992.

Poirot-Delpech, Bertrand, *Diagonales*. Paris: Gallimard, 1995.

Polanyi, Karl, *Origins of Our Time: The Great Transformation*. London, 1944.

Pol Droit, Roger, *L'Avenir aujourd'hui dépend-il de nous?* Paris: Le Monde éditions, 1995.

Ramonet, Ignacio, 'Pouvoirs fin de siècle'. *Le Monde diplomatique* (March 1995).

Rancière, Jacques, *La Mésentente (politique et philosophie)*. Paris: Galilée, 1987.

Reich, Robert B., *The Work of Nations: Preparing Ourselves for 21st Century*

Capitalism. New York: Alfred A. Knopf, Inc., 1991.

Revel, Jean-François *Le Regain démocratique*, Paris: Fayard, 1992.

Rifkin, Jeremy, *The End of Work*. New York: Putnam, 1995.

Rigaudiat, Jacques, *Réduire le temps de travail*. Paris: Syros, 1993.

Rosenvallon, Pierre, *La Nouvelle Question sociale*. Paris: Seuil, 1995.

Rousselet, Jean, *L'Allergie au travail*. Paris: Seuil, 1978.

Rousselet, Micheline, *Les Tiers-Mondes*. Paris: Le Monde-Marabout, 1994.

Roustang, Guy, Laville, Jean-Louis, Eme, Bernard, Mothé, Daniel and Perret, Bernard, *Vers un nouveau contrat social*. Paris: Desclée de Brouwer, 1996.

Séguin, Philippe, *En attendant l'emploi . . .* Paris: Seuil, 1996.

Shakespeare, William, *The Tempest*, ed. Frank Kermode. London: Methuen (The Arden Shakespeare), 1954.

Suleiman, Ezra N., *Les Raisons cachées de la réussite française*. Paris: Seuil, 1995.

Sullerot, Evelyne, *L'Age de travailler*. Paris: Fayard, 1986.

Supiot, Alain, *Critique du droit du travail*. Paris: PUF, 1994.

Thuillier, Pierre, *La Grande Implosion*. Paris: Fayard, 1995.

Todd, Emmanuel, *Le Destin des immigrés: assimilation et ségrégation dans les démocraties occidentales*. Paris: Seuil, 1994.

Toffler, Alvin, *Powershift*. New York: Bantam Books, 1990.

Topalov, Christian, *Naissance du chômeur (1880–1910)*. Paris: Albin Michel, 1994.

Touraine, Alain, *Production de la société*. Paris: Seuil, 1973. In English: *The Self-Production of Society*, trans. Derek Coltman. Chicago: University of Chicago Press, 1977.

Touraine, Alain, *Critique de la modernité*. Paris: Fayard, 1992. In English: *Critique of Modernity*, trans. David Macey. Oxford: Blackwell, 1995.

Touraine, Alain, *Qu'est que la démocratie?* Paris: Fayard, 1994.

Touraine, Alain, Dubet, François, Lapeyronnie, Didier, Khosrokhavar, Farhad and Wieviorka, Michel, *Le Grand Refus. Réflexions sur la grève de décembre 1995*. Paris: Fayard, 1996.

Tribalat, Michèle (with Simon, Patrick and Riandey, Benoît), *De l'immigration à l'assimilation*. Paris: La Decouverte, 1996.

Vaillant, Emmanuel, *L'Immigration*. Paris: Milan, 1996.

Vetz, Pierre, *Mondialisation des villes et des territoires, l'économie d'archipel*. Paris: PUF, 1996.

Virilio, Paul, *Cybermonde, la politique du pire* (Conversations with Philippe Petit). Paris: Textuel, 1996.

Voyer, Jean-Pierre, *Une enquête sur la nature et les causes de la misère des gens*. Paris: Lebovici, 1976.

Warde, Ibrahim, 'La Dérive des nouveaux produits financiers'. *Le Monde diplomatique* (July 1994).

Wiener, Norbert, 'Cybernetics, or Control and Communication' in *The Man and the Machine*. 1948.

Wiener, Norbert, 'The Human Use of Human Beings', in *Cybernetics and Human Beings*. 1950.

Wuhl, Simon, *Les Exclus face à l'emploi*. Paris: Syros, 1992.